# Journey to
# Contentment

**The Bible Reading Fellowship**
15 The Chambers, Vineyard
Abingdon OX14 3FE
**brf.org.uk**

The Bible Reading Fellowship (BRF) is a Registered Charity (233280)

ISBN 978 0 85746 592 4
First published 2020
10 9 8 7 6 5 4 3 2 1 0
All rights reserved

**Acknowledgements**
Unless otherwise acknowledged, scripture quotations are taken from The
New Revised Standard Version of the Bible, Anglicised edition, copyright ©
1989, 1995 by the Division of Christian Education of the National Council of
the Churches of Christ in the United States of America. Used by permission. All
rights reserved. • Scripture quotation marked NIV is taken from The Holy Bible,
New International Version (Anglicised edition) copyright © 1979, 1984, 2011
by Biblica. Used by permission of Hodder & Stoughton Publishers, a Hachette
UK company. All rights reserved. 'NIV' is a registered trademark of Biblica. UK
trademark number 1448790. • Scripture quotations marked KJV are taken from
the Authorised Version of the Bible (The King James Bible), the rights in which
are vested in the Crown. Reproduced by permission of the Crown's Patentee,
Cambridge University Press. • Scripture quotation marked ESV is taken from the
Holy Bible, English Standard Version, published by HarperCollins Publishers, ©
2001 Crossway Bibles, a division of Good News Publishers. Used by permission.
All rights reserved. • Scripture quotation marked ASV is taken from the American
Standard Version, which is in the public domain.

Every effort has been made to trace and contact copyright owners for material
used in this resource. We apologise for any inadvertent omissions or errors, and
would ask those concerned to contact us so that full acknowledgement can be
made in the future.

A catalogue record for this book is available from the British Library

Printed and bound by CPI Group (UK) Ltd, Croydon CR0 4YY

Sally Welch

# Journey to Contentment

**Pilgrimage principles
for everyday life**

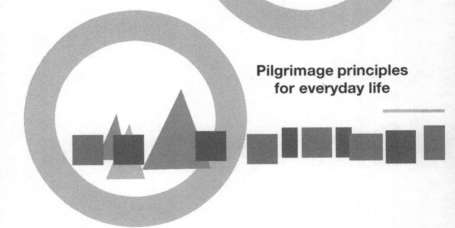

# Contents

# Introduction

One of the most joyful parts of my ministry is leading pilgrimages. These journeys are usually for one day, although occasionally I lead them over a number of days. Before they begin, I will have worked out the route and walked it at least once. I will have planned what I want to say once we are on the pilgrimage: where to stop, when to eat, how to pray and what sort of conversations and reflections I want to encourage. On the day of the pilgrimage itself, I will pray for the events of the journey, for my travelling companions and for myself, that through this activity we might learn more about ourselves, about each other and about God. To this extent, I am the leader of the pilgrimage, the guide. Once on the journey, however, I am also a fellow pilgrim. I may walk at the front, to help lead the party along the chosen route, but I also walk alongside, sharing insights, experiencing the highs and lows of the journey and growing in knowledge and wisdom.

In writing this book, I have taken the responsibility of leading the party of readers; I have undertaken the research, reflected on the scripture and mined my own experience and that of others for insights and wisdom. However, I am also on the journey myself, a fellow traveller along the route to contentment. When I told my family I was writing a book about contentment, they looked at me askance and the silent question appeared in their eyes: 'What authority do you have to write this?' I answered them out loud: 'I am writing this book because I too seek contentment, and I want to share my findings with others as I share my journey with them.'

I hope you will find help and support for your journey in this book; I pray that your experience of contentment will broaden and deepen; I ask your forgiveness for the ways in which I will fail, even as I struggle to teach; I rejoice in the invisible companionship of others, held together in their engagement with this book, as we travel together, accompanied by one another and by Christ, who is the beginning and the end and the companion of all our journeys.

This book is divided into 52 sections of a journey, beginning with the preparations necessary before setting out, then exploring the obstacles which might be put in our path and sharing ways in which the journey can be made easier and more productive. At the end of each reflection, there is a suggestion for an activity or a prayer. Not all these exercises will suit everybody – some will want to try every one; others will prefer to select only those they feel are most helpful.

As I wrote this book, the image that returned to me again and again was that of one of the most famous pilgrims of all time – Christian, the main character of John Bunyan's book *The Pilgrim's Progress*. Written at the end of the 17th century, the book tells the story of Christian, who, bearing the knowledge of his personal sin as a pack upon his back, feels impelled to make the journey from the City of Destruction to the Celestial City. As he travels, Christian encounters many characters, some of whom help and others who hinder him on his journey. He makes his way through the allegorical places of the Slough of Despond and the Valley of the Shadow of Death, learning more about himself and his faith, before he finally arrives at the Celestial City.

In my mind's eye, Christian is a lonely figure, plodding steadfastly on, eyes fixed firmly on his goal, facing bravely the dangers and adventures of the road, confident that his final destination is the right one. Although often distracted and sometimes deterred, he never ceases on his journey, and it is this determination which encouraged me during the writing process and which I hope will be part of your journey also. You may choose to study a section of this book every day; you may find you need more time to reflect or you have less time for study, and therefore must leave a gap of two or three days or even a week between each section. But in order to benefit most, you must persevere – perhaps, like Christian, finding the way difficult at times, but never ceasing to strive towards your destination.

God of green pastures and still waters, rocks and wilderness –
you show me the path of life.
Help me to follow in your ways,
trusting in your merciful goodness and purposes for me,
alive in the knowledge and love of your Son,
who is the Way, the Truth and the Life.
Amen

# Section I

## Before we begin

In *The Pilgrim's Progress*, Christian begins his journey in great haste. Told by the Evangelist the direction in which he must travel in order to escape 'from the wrath to come', Christian sets off at a run, not heeding his wife and children and various neighbours who follow after him, trying to dissuade him from his course.

Our journey to contentment should have a more measured start. A journey of any significant length, whether spiritual or physical, requires some preparation before setting off, not only so a good start can be made, but so the journey can be continued and finished satisfactorily as well.

This first section introduces some things which will hopefully help you on your way – prayer and study habits, a right attitude of mind and a determination to gain as much as possible from the journey ahead.

# I have learned

I rejoice in the Lord greatly that now at last you have revived your concern for me; indeed, you were concerned for me, but had no opportunity to show it. Not that I am referring to being in need; for I have learned to be content with whatever I have. I know what it is to have little, and I know what it is to have plenty. In any and all circumstances I have learned the secret of being well-fed and of going hungry, of having plenty and of being in need. I can do all things through him who strengthens me.

PHILIPPIANS 4:10–13

My eldest daughter is an enthusiastic amateur actress – and fortunately her talent matches her enthusiasm. When she was only 13, I promised her that she could have her ears pierced if she won the leading role in the school play, thinking that this was highly unlikely given the number of older, more experienced pupils who were also auditioning for the main part. Two days later we were choosing ear studs! Since then, she has gone from Cordelia to Lady Macbeth, Helena to Portia (she has a passion for Shakespeare). My husband and I watch as many of her plays as we can, marvelling at the way that the tiny bundle of energy we brought home from hospital on Boxing Day has grown into a woman who can get inside the nature of so many characters, transforming herself with such apparent ease into an old crone, a young girl or a sick and bitter woman. But we know that the ease with which she takes on the personality and character of another is not without effort, for we have also been witnesses to the hours of patient learning of lines, the evenings spent in draughty rehearsal rooms and the painstaking activity of working out who will move where and when on stage. The work is repaid as her audience is transported into another world, there to discover more about people and relationships and perhaps also themselves.

I could have used the example of a musician whose joyful notes hide the hours of solitary practice, a footballer whose skill at placing the ball is the reward for hours of work on cold pitches or the linguist whose fluent conversation is the result of learning verb declensions by heart. All these skills, so admired by the rest of us for the ease with which they are performed, hide much effort and hard work. Sometimes the learning is a joyful process, but there will inevitably be times when willpower is all that prevents the learner from giving up in despair. And it seems to me that for us the process of learning becomes harder – we are more secure with what we do know and perhaps less willing to embark on the adventure of the unknown, with its promise of uncertainty. Skilled at some things, we are reluctant to start right back at the beginning again, experiencing once more those first faltering steps on the way to gaining a new accomplishment. Our brains, too, it seems, have become less flexible, our time more limited – we like to be certain of results before we invest in a new endeavour. So it is not surprising, perhaps, that we read those three words of Paul with some trepidation: 'I have learned.' We know that what follows is the result of some effort, of hard work, of failures as well as successes, of slow progress as well as sudden inspiration. But we also know that because of those three words, what is being shared with us is of great value, because Paul considered it worth the effort: 'I have learned to be content with whatever I have.'

Contentment is not a secret, but it is a mystery. The state of contentment is achieved with grace, but it is not given as a gift – it is learned, and the lessons can be hard work. Contentment is not something which can be assumed or faked, and we quickly spot those who merely seem to have achieved it. The glib assertions that a person 'doesn't need much to be content' or is 'happy with only a little' are betrayed by an anxious restlessness or a half-hidden yearning. They show, too, a misunderstanding of the nature of contentment – it is not merely a willingness to be happy with what one has been given, however meagre that amount is. Contentment is a profound spiritual act, a way of living and being which combines an acceptance of all that God provides with a desire to move ever deeper into relationship with the creator. Contentment is born of an attitude of trust in the purposes of God for each one of us and a willingness to step out boldly into the unknown for the sake of his kingdom.

We must begin our journey to contentment with an attitude of humility, willing to learn – however challenging that act of learning will be. We must be prepared to work hard and suffer setbacks, but with the knowledge that such setbacks are not the end of the journey, only obstacles along the way, and that the prize is truly worth the effort.

## Exercise

Spend some time reflecting on the things you have learned over your life. Try to make a list of them. It might help to divide the list into different areas – things you have learned about the way other people behave, skills you have acquired, experiences you have had which have led to wisdom or insight. Choose one or two, and try to remember what it felt like to be a beginner, just setting out on the path to learning. Remember the successes and the setbacks, and the feelings that each brought. Try to recapture that attitude of determination and excitement which heralds the start of a new project – and put it towards this new venture of learning contentment.

# From the darkness

Now there was a good and righteous man named Joseph, who, though a member of the council, had not agreed to their plan and action. He came from the Jewish town of Arimathea, and he was waiting expectantly for the kingdom of God. This man went to Pilate and asked for the body of Jesus. Then he took it down, wrapped it in a linen cloth, and laid it in a rock-hewn tomb where no one had ever been laid. It was the day of Preparation, and the sabbath was beginning. The women who had come with him from Galilee followed, and they saw the tomb and how his body was laid. Then they returned, and prepared spices and ointments.

LUKE 23:50–56

My husband has always been an outdoorsy type – right from the beginning of our relationship, going on a date involved fewer evenings spent in restaurants and theatres and more days spent climbing mountains and going on long walks in wild places. And it wasn't long before he introduced me to the joys of caving or potholing. Wearing a bright-green helmet, an ill-fitting, borrowed set of overalls and a pair of strong wellington boots, we trudged across what seemed like miles of rough Yorkshire hillside to insert ourselves into the narrow passageways which led deep underground. Nervously following the man whom I didn't yet know very well, I wondered what I had let myself in for, as I bumped my helmet yet again on a piece of rock protruding from the tunnel-like formation we were exploring. Reaching a larger cave, we sat for a moment to regain our breath, and my husband-to-be told me to turn off my head torch just to see how dark it was. The blackness that surrounded me was the deepest I have ever known. There was not a tiny fraction of light, not even a softening of the dense darkness that seemed almost physical. Sitting there, it seemed as if even my body didn't exist, since I was aware only of how it felt, not what it looked like – my eyes were open but I could see nothing. After a few moments, we turned our head torches back on and the world made sense once more, but the memory of that first experience of total darkness has stayed with me for over 30 years.

How dark the tomb must have been once that stone was rolled over the entrance! How deep and despairing were the thoughts and emotions of those whose hopes were buried with the body of their beloved teacher in that space filled only by a blackness darker than night, without the faintest glimmer of hope. Yet it is from within that very darkness that the story of the saving of the world found its conclusion and its new beginning. Just when it seemed as if hope had been extinguished, a new hope was born, one which included all people for all time. Through the confusion of the trial, the poison of plotting and betrayal, the manipulation of ordinary people by those in power, God's will was done. Through the pain and the loss and the weeping and the agony, God's purposes were achieved. Out of oppression and fear, darkness and misery, a new way of living begins, one which is filled with light and love and the certain hope of salvation.

So we begin our journey towards contentment – from the darkness of our selfish lives, aware of our frailties but unable, so often, to prevent ourselves from falling into temptation, struggling towards the light. But always we have the knowledge that Christ has been there before us; he has explored the very depths of the tomb, inhabited the darkness which knows no light, in order to bring light to humankind.

# Exercise

If you can, find a place which is totally dark. This may simply be a room in your house at night, but the experience will be more powerful if it is somewhere which is slightly unsettling. You might find somewhere in a church building, for example, or out in a wood or open space, or simply stand outside in your garden. Make sure wherever you are is safe, however, and that you do not put yourself or others at risk. Take a torch or a candle with you, but ensure also that you have access to a brighter, more stable source of light.

Spend some time experiencing the darkness. Explore your surroundings using your other senses – see what a difference is made to them by the absence of sight. After a few moments, light your candle or turn on your torch. How have your surroundings changed? Notice how the darkness seems even darker near the light, but also how your eyes are drawn to the light and the feeling of safety it brings.

'My eyes have seen your salvation, which you have prepared in the presence of all peoples, a light for revelation to the Gentiles and for glory to your people Israel.'
LUKE 2:30–32

# Don't look among the dead

But on the first day of the week, at early dawn, they came to the tomb, taking the spices that they had prepared. They found the stone rolled away from the tomb, but when they went in, they did not find the body. While they were perplexed about this, suddenly two men in dazzling clothes stood beside them. The women were terrified and bowed their faces to the ground, but the men said to them, 'Why do you look for the living among the dead? He is not here, but has risen.'

LUKE 24:1–5

A service of light, particularly one that takes place in a large church or cathedral, is a wonderful event. Beginning before dawn on Easter morning, the congregation might gather outside and begin the service in the cold and dark. At sunrise, a fire is kindled and a new paschal candle is blessed and lit from it. The candle is then taken into the unlit church, while the ministers and congregation follow in procession. Further candles are lit from the paschal candle until the whole building is ablaze with light and the risen Jesus is proclaimed.

Those of us who stand outside in the cold and the dark are lucky – we know it will not be long before we encounter the light and are allowed in to the warmth. The visitors to the tomb on that first Easter Day were not so fortunate; they believed that their time in the light was over forever and all they had to look forward to was endless darkness. We who know the happy ending of the gospel can only just begin to imagine the feelings of loneliness and despair of those who came with spices to anoint the body of their beloved master. And then, it seems, even that comforting task, that last service that they can offer to the one they loved, is taken away from them. But they are not left to suffer long, as the 'two men in dazzling clothes' address them with words which must have seemed quite stern to those who were in shock and grief: 'Why do you look for the living among the dead?'

Why were they there? How slight was their faith! After all the teaching and the conversations, all the miracles and the time spent in the presence of the Son of God, they still sought Jesus among the dead. And how comforting for us, as we, like those first witnesses to the resurrection, so often get it wrong. We, like them, lack faith, fail to hear God's purposes, look for Jesus among the dead and not the risen.

As we prepare for our journey towards contentment, as we leave the darkness of unbelief and the loneliness of our fear and doubt, we can return again and again to the knowledge that our journey will not be undertaken alone. Wherever we go, however dark it seems, however fearful the wilderness, we can travel in the knowledge that Christ has gone before us. However far from the path we stray, there is nowhere that has not been visited and blessed by the light of Christ, brought into the world on that first Easter Day, and celebrated every moment ever since by the whole of creation. We must make up our minds to walk in the light, to rejoice in the living – not to look among the dead things of past regrets and errors, of wrongs committed and good not undertaken. We will not find Jesus among our actions of former times, for he is risen and lives with us now, walking alongside us as we journey, supporting us, encouraging us, always loving us.

## Exercise

At the beginning of your journey to contentment, hold your own darkness-into-light event. Begin before dawn, or as early as you can, and spend some time in darkness. You do not have to actively pray or think – simply rest in the presence of God. When you have spent enough time doing this, light a candle and watch it burn for a while. Imagine yourself travelling to the tomb that first morning, in the darkness of pre-dawn, disappointed and frightened. What will your reactions be when you see that the tomb is empty and, instead of your beloved teacher's body, there are two angels! What do you feel as you listen to their words?

Gradually make your space lighter, either by adding more candles or simply turning on the light. Remember that you now walk in the light, that your journey is never a solitary one and that Jesus is with you wherever you go. If you wish, you can write 'Why do you look for the living among the dead? He is not here, but has risen' and place it somewhere you will see it every day, a constant reminder of your companion.

# For the gate is narrow

'Enter through the narrow gate; for the gate is wide and the road is easy that leads to destruction, and there are many who take it. For the gate is narrow and the road is hard that leads to life, and there are few who find it.'
MATTHEW 7:13–14

There are few things more dispiriting than the experience of sharing a plan or project with a friend or colleague and, instead of receiving a reaction of interest and encouragement, being told all the difficulties and downfalls that might be associated with such an enterprise. There are, it seems, some people in the world who specialise in that sort of response – when we look for support or enthusiasm, we are given discouragement and a list of all the things that might go wrong. The temptation is to avoid these people for fear that they will discourage us to such an extent that we no longer dare to carry out our plans. It's far easier to spend time with those who encourage us in our projects, who offer us practical help and advice or encouraging words, which make the planning and execution of our task a more enjoyable prospect.

Certainly, the words of Jesus concerning our journey towards the kingdom of heaven are not encouraging – the road will be difficult and might be unpleasant; we may be tempted to go astray and choose an easier path which leads us in the wrong direction; certainly the future is fraught and the outcome uncertain. The temptation for us may well be to decide before we start that the journey will be too challenging for us, and we should give up before we even begin, so slender are the chances of success. We might feel that it is better by far to put aside these warning words, along with those of our pessimistic friends, and turn instead to others who have a more cheerful outlook.

In some cases, however, the warnings and gloomy forecasts which our less optimistic friends might offer can be useful, or even vital – if we are about to undertake something difficult or dangerous for which we are ill-prepared – and we would do well to take them seriously. If we are unaware of the possible negative outcomes that we might face, it is important that those around us who have experience of a similar undertaking warn us of the challenges we might encounter, so that we can be prepared for them. Better by far to prepare for all eventualities than be dismayed to the point of giving up when we first encounter difficulties.

So we can take Jesus' words seriously and apply them to our self-made challenge of learning contentment. The journey will not be easy, and the temptation to turn aside and choose an easier task, a more achievable goal, may well be great. But if we are prepared for challenges, we will have the determination to overcome them; if we acknowledge that there may be difficulties ahead, we will not be surprised when we meet them. And always we are reminded that it is on the hard path, through the narrow gate, that we will meet Jesus.

## Exercise

> You can never cross the ocean unless you have the courage to lose sight of the shore.
>
> André Gide

What might this quote be saying to you right now? What things are there in your life which might prevent you from leading the life God is calling you to live? As you set out on this spiritual adventure, are you prepared in your heart and mind for the challenges you will meet? What sort of things do you think they will be? Which habits and attitudes might you be called to leave behind?

If you wish, find or draw a picture of an ocean shore. Draw yourself standing on the shore, and draw or write down all the things which might be preventing you from setting out on your spiritual journey. Are they practical things like finding time within a day for reading and praying, or are there anxieties about the process of the journey, or a fear of 'failing'? Draw the boat you will get in. Who is in the boat with you?

# Where are you?

**They heard the sound of the Lord God walking in the garden at the time of the evening breeze, and the man and his wife hid themselves from the presence of the Lord God among the trees of the garden. But the Lord God called to the man, and said to him, 'Where are you?'**

GENESIS 3:8–9

Usually when I look after my grandson, we remain in the house and the garden. One day, however, due to the unexpected nature of the visit, we had to visit the supermarket to buy lunch. This was a very exciting expedition, and we were both overwhelmed by the choice of biscuits available – and at such a convenient height as well! I turned around briefly to transfer three or four packets from my basket back to the shelves, and when I turned back, my grandson had gone. That heart-stopping moment of realisation will be painfully familiar to almost every parent or grandparent, as well as the unspeakable relief when he was discovered at the end of the aisle, quietly exploring an open packet of doughnuts.

There are other, more significant, times in our lives when we call out, 'Where are you?' We may be singing out into the future, seeking a partner or friend with whom to share our lives, uncertain where that person may be or whether they will ever make themselves known. We may be looking back into the past, remembering times spent with those we love but see no longer – lonely sighs during the dark watches of the night, hoping in the promise of a future meeting but missing the reality of human touch and companionship. We may be calling out in anger to our God, who in times of deepest despair and agony might seem to be absent, or at least so well hidden that his presence cannot be perceived.

But here, in the garden of Eden, things are different. Although God has not been apparent during the day, his absence has not been regretted or missed. It might have gone better for Adam and Eve if it had been – if they had paused and looked round for God or called out for him, they might have saved themselves. In that moment of hesitation, of looking, there might have crept an awareness of the nature of the actions they contemplated. Instead of listening to the voice of the serpent, they might have listened for the voice of their creator and made a different choice. But they do not call out, 'Where are you?', and God respects their decision, asking only that they in their turn accept the consequences. And at the end of the day, at the time of the evening breeze, it is God who seeks them, making the first step towards realisation, acceptance and finally reconciliation.

How important it is to remember this – that from the very beginning it is God who makes the first move, God who seeks us, God who stands at the door knocking. All we are required to do is acknowledge that yearning and respond to it, turning towards God, who has been there all the time and is simply waiting for us to see him.

## Exercise

Spend some time reflecting on where you are in your life right now. Look at different aspects of your life – your home situation, your occupations, your emotional state. Where are you in these? Are you in a comfortable, stable place, or do you feel unsettled, insecure? Are there adjustments and alterations that need to be made? Is the balance between different aspects of your life a healthy one, or are some areas being neglected and others over-energised? If God met you walking in the garden of Eden, what would you want to say about your current position?

Draw a map of your spiritual journey. Using pictures or words, write or illustrate the high points and the low ones you have experienced in your relationship with God. You might want to think about times of faith and doubt, times when God revealed his presence to you and times when it seemed he was absent. Picture yourself at the beginning of a new stage. What are you looking towards? Where do you hope to be?

# Section II

## Stepping out in faith

With our mental and spiritual bags packed, we set off, travelling as lightly as possible, leaving only traces of our journey behind us, in true pilgrim fashion. This section encourages us to look carefully at the baggage we are taking with us, both material and emotional, and encourages an attitude of cheerful abstinence, paring down the contents of our daily lives to the bare essentials, thus leaving more space for God. Although Christian's departure was over-hasty, we are reminded that by putting off a good action until the next day, we cease to engage with that good action and it becomes merely a notion in the future, helpful to no one.

# Nothing for the journey

> He called the twelve and began to send them out two by two, and gave them authority over the unclean spirits. He ordered them to take nothing for their journey except a staff; no bread, no bag, no money in their belts; but to wear sandals and not to put on two tunics.
>
> MARK 6:7–9

As part of my work, I give lectures and workshops on pilgrimage – both the practical and spiritual aspects of this activity. Pilgrimage is a spiritual journey to a sacred place, and I explore what this means, the history of pilgrimage and the way a pilgrimage might be undertaken today. I discuss the importance of making a good preparation for pilgrimage, as one would for any journey – as one would for the journey to contentment, in fact – and above all, I emphasise the importance of packing well and travelling light.

Following the example of Jesus' instructions to his followers as they set out on their all-important mission to bring the good news of humankind's salvation through the loving grace of God to all people, I urge a spartan approach to packing. I have seen too many journeys crippled almost from the start by the pilgrim's enthusiastic embrace of every type of device and new piece of equipment. Designed to make the journey easier, all these do is weigh down the walker, adding another obstacle to the successful completion of the journey. Although I would never advocate the extreme of taking no luggage at all, certainly 'less is best' is my motto.

But Jesus' words are aimed not just at those first few disciples-turned-missionaries; they are directed at all of us who wish to follow Jesus and share his message with others, whether we travel far and wide or whether we spend our efforts within one community or area. Again and again, we are urged by Jesus to live lightly to the things of the world, for fear they will weigh us down when embarking on our spiritual journey and become obstacles to our relationship with God and with our fellow human beings. We are reminded that the man who builds a bigger barn to store his overflow of grain may die in the night (Luke 12:16–21). We witness the rich man reject Jesus' teaching because it is easier than rejecting his own wealth (Matthew 19:16–24). We are taught not that material possessions are in themselves bad, but that care for them can become our main priority, distracting us from God and neighbour. So we are urged to put our faith in God, not things, and trust in his good provision for us: 'Make purses for yourselves that do not wear out, an unfailing treasure in heaven, where no thief comes near and no moth destroys' (Luke 12:33).

But there is a still deeper message for us in Jesus' teaching – just as we must travel lightly through the material world, so we endeavour not to weigh ourselves down with spiritual burdens either. We must leave behind our regrets for the past and not concern ourselves with the possibilities of the future, for these are in God's hands: 'So do not worry about tomorrow, for tomorrow will bring worries of its own. Today's trouble is enough for today' (Matthew 6:34). Instead, we begin our journey with optimism and faith, concerned only with the necessities of life, and confident in God's good provision for us: 'Therefore do not worry, saying, "What will we eat?" or "What will we drink?" or "What will we wear?" For it is the Gentiles who strive for all these things; and indeed your heavenly Father knows that you need all these things. But strive first for the kingdom of God and his righteousness, and all these things will be given to you as well' (Matthew 6:31–33).

## Exercise

'Take no gold, or silver, or copper in your belts, no bag for your journey, or two tunics, or sandals, or a staff.'
MATTHEW 10:9–10

A useful exercise when considering our possessions is to undertake to get rid of one every day. This can be a small object or a large one – something which has not been used for a while, perhaps, or an unwanted gift. Look in your cupboards and attics – you may surprise yourself with what is there! Be thoughtful about disposing of your possessions. Can they go to a charity shop or be donated to a fundraising event? Only as a last resort should they be recycled or destroyed. To begin with, this may be difficult; as you continue, you should feel relieved of the burden of caring for so many possessions. You might want to journal how you feel about this. If there are objects to which you have an emotional attachment but no practical use for, why not take a photograph and make an album of them? This will use much less space but still provide memories of people and places.

# First let me bury my father

[Jesus] said, 'Follow me.' But he said, 'Lord, first let me go and bury my father.' But Jesus said to him, 'Let the dead bury their own dead; but as for you, go and proclaim the kingdom of God.' Another said, 'I will follow you, Lord; but let me first say farewell to those at my home.' Jesus said to him, 'No one who puts a hand to the plough and looks back is fit for the kingdom of God.'

LUKE 9:59–62

Jesus has set his face towards Jerusalem. He knows where he has to go to fulfil his purpose – but do his followers? The three people he meets on this part of the journey have different responses to Jesus' call to follow him. The first is full of enthusiasm, even when Jesus reminds him that the journey will be challenging and that by his action he will be leaving behind all that is stable and secure. The second and third men, however, both have commitments at home, duties and responsibilities which they must first discharge before they are able to follow Jesus, as they long to do. Burying one's father was a serious obligation, part of the Jewish tradition of honouring one's parents, obeying the fifth commandment. It would seem to be a valid excuse, but Jesus is adamant – if the path of life is not chosen, then you might as well be as dead as your father, he responds. The third would-be follower simply wishes to say goodbye to his loved ones. He is following the example of Elisha, who before he follows Elijah first kisses his parents goodbye: 'He left the oxen, ran after

Elijah, and said, "Let me kiss my father and my mother, and then I will follow you"' (1 Kings 19:20). But Jesus' response is the same – you can't go forwards in a straight line if you are looking back all the time.

Most of us who try to follow Jesus have commitments and obligations which are important not only to us, but also to those with whom we live and those whom we serve. It would be not only harsh but also a direct disobedience to Jesus' command to love our neighbour as ourselves if we were to put aside all those people and activities to which we have given our love and service in order to follow Jesus. However, we are being reminded in this passage that we must take care not to allow our relationships with others to block or obstruct our relationship with God – that true, perfect relationship from which all others flow.

As we set out on our journey to contentment, let us make sure not only that we have lightened ourselves of physical burdens which might weigh us down, but that we are emotionally and spiritually prepared for the difficult task ahead of us. We can take time to reassess those people and activities towards which we have obligations, and discern whether there is a genuine call for us to undertake this work of love or whether this call is now past. Try to be honest about your motives – are you using some tasks and events as an excuse for not following Christ as you should? Are you hiding behind commitments which are unnecessary or could even be undertaken better by others?

## Exercise

Gather together a pen and some stones – a handful or two should be enough. Draw or cut out some heart shapes from paper or card.

Taking a stone in your hands, think of an emotional responsibility or concern you have. This may be for another person – a child, a sick relative or a friend who is dependent on you. It may also be for a group or activity you are committed to, which depends upon your help or support.

Think about this responsibility and pray for God's wisdom in deciding whether this is a genuine call to which you must respond. You might feel that it is indeed a commitment which God has called you to fulfil, but it is worth considering whether the commitment is still valid or has become outdated, or whether other people might be better able to fulfil this than you.

When you have finished, take the pile of stones, which represent burdens that you feel can be laid down, and hand over responsibility for them completely to God. You may want to do this stone by stone or as a group. Turn aside from this pile of stones now.

Taking those stones which symbolise your current emotional burdens, ask God for the strength to carry them and the grace to turn them from burdens into joys, from responsibilities into caring partnerships – working with God and the people involved to transform the situations concerned. As you pray, place each stone upon a heart. When you have finished, move the stones away until you are left simply with the hearts.

Jesus' warning that the proverbial camel, likely laden down with goods, cannot squeeze through the 'eye of the needle' applies not only to the materially encumbered; we must lay down any unnecessary burdens – so that we may pass freely into heaven. For all we need is given to us as a gift of grace.

# Now is a good time

The Egyptians urged the people to hasten their departure from the land, for they said, 'We shall all be dead'... The Israelites journeyed from Rameses to Succoth, about six hundred thousand men on foot, besides children. A mixed crowd also went up with them, and livestock in great numbers, both flocks and herds. They baked unleavened cakes of the dough that they had brought out of Egypt; it was not leavened, because they were driven out of Egypt and could not wait, nor had they prepared any provisions for themselves.

EXODUS 12:33, 37–39

Some very good friends of mine have spent most of their adult lives trying to buy a house in France. Originally it was because they planned to live there for a few years, while the children were young, in order to give everyone the experience of living in a different country and to gain the skill of speaking French fluently. As time went on and the children grew, this idea became impractical, but my friends were fortunate in their jobs and salaries and decided they would like to buy a small holiday cottage in France instead. Many joyful holidays and weekends were spent house-hunting in different areas of the country, but still nothing was purchased. The houses were never quite right, never quite fitted the image which the couple held in their minds of the perfect house. When I saw them a few months ago, they had retired to a cottage in Wells. I asked them about their dream of a French house, and the woman smiled wryly. 'It was never the right time,' she said. 'And now the time has run out.'

It is a witness of God's good timing that the Israelites were given so little warning about leaving Egypt. Otherwise I am sure the challenges of packing up a lifetime's goods and possessions, of settling business and domestic affairs and of making travel arrangements would have been so complicated that they might never have left! But the children of Israel were forced to move fast – so fast that not even the supplies of bread that were needed for the journey could be properly prepared but had to be baked before they could rise.

The annual re-enactment of this occasion, celebrated at the festival of the Passover, serves as a reminder to us all that nothing should stand in the way of following God's will. Human beings are very good at putting off difficult or unpleasant tasks, or tasks requiring energy and effort, even if we know that the results will be good for us or for those around us. We are similarly prone to put off spiritual exercises or challenges. We may not be aware of God's good purposes for us; we may wish to postpone a spiritual exercise or practice that we fear may be too demanding or challenging for us. We may spend much time in making preparations for a time of reflection or study, without ever getting down to the activity itself. But just as the Israelites gathered everything together and left as soon as was practical, so too must we stop prevaricating and begin this journey which we have decided upon. We will never be sufficiently prepared, but we will find what we need along the way, for God will be travelling with us and will provide for all our needs.

## Exercise

Take your diary, calendar or whatever helps you to schedule your time and sit with it in a quiet place. This may be your prayer space if you have one, or simply a space where you are free to pray and to reflect undisturbed. Look through the events and activities that you have planned for the next few weeks. It may help also if you write in those tasks which you carry out daily or frequently and don't bother to put in your diary – helping a friend, doing the housework or shopping, attending church. Think about the rhythm of your day; when is the best time for you to be quiet and reflective? Some people do this best at the very beginning of the day, before the rest of the household is awake, others prefer to pray and think at the very end of the day. Choose the time which suits you best, which sees you with most energy. It might help if you write this time into your diary or find another way to make yourself accountable for keeping this time. Ask God to help you dedicate this time to him and to this journey.

> For [God] says, 'At an acceptable time I have listened to you, and on a day of salvation I have helped you.' See, now is the acceptable time; see, now is the day of salvation!
>
> 2 CORINTHIANS 6:2

# Don't look back

When morning dawned, the angels urged Lot, saying, 'Get up, take your wife and your two daughters who are here, or else you will be consumed in the punishment of the city.' But he lingered; so the men seized him and his wife and his two daughters by the hand, the Lord being merciful to him, and they brought him out and left him outside the city. When they had brought them outside, they said, 'Flee for your life; do not look back or stop anywhere in the Plain; flee to the hills, or else you will be consumed.' And Lot said to them, 'Oh, no, my lords; your servant has found favour with you, and you have shown me great kindness in saving my life; but I cannot flee to the hills, for fear the disaster will overtake me and I die. Look, that city is near enough to flee to, and it is a little one. Let me escape there – is it not a little one? – and my life will be saved!' He said to him, 'Very well, I grant you this favour too, and will not overthrow the city of which you have spoken. Hurry, escape there, for I can do nothing until you arrive there.' Therefore the city was called Zoar. The sun had risen on the earth when Lot came to Zoar.

Then the Lord rained on Sodom and Gomorrah sulphur and fire from the Lord out of heaven; and he overthrew those cities, and all the Plain, and all the inhabitants of the cities, and what grew on the ground. But Lot's wife, behind him, looked back, and she became a pillar of salt.

GENESIS 19:15–26

Poor Lot's wife! Known throughout the world – yet no one knows her name. Her fame is confined solely to her inability to follow instructions and the appalling fate she suffered because of that. But if we read the paragraph before, a paragraph which is so often overlooked when telling the story of God's destruction of Sodom and Gomorrah, we learn that Lot too had his moment of wavering. In fact, it wasn't Lot who fled the city at all – the angels had to take hold of the family and physically transport them to safety! Even then, Lot argued over the method of salvation, pleading to be allowed to flee to a city rather than into the hills because that seemed much easier.

It is usual when embarking on any major enterprise that we should have doubts and anxieties. It is sensible, in fact – if we were not aware of the risks and possible dangers of a new undertaking, there is the chance that we might underestimate the effort and time needed for the task and set ourselves up for failure before we have even begun. But there comes a time when the research has all been done, the questions have all been asked and answers have been found. Then is the time for action – action without regret or backward glances. Of course, we must always be ready to change our plans if new information or circumstances come to light, but we must keep pressing forwards if the race is to be won.

My eldest son recently changed careers, from a 'safe' position with job security and good working conditions to one which was far riskier but also where his heart lay. Before he did so, he had long discussions with people he knew and trusted about the wisdom of such a move. He talked about his reasons for leaving, the advantages of the new post and also how he might feel in different situations – if he were offered more money or a promotion in order to stay in his current post, for example. Only when he had worked many different scenarios did he hand in his notice. He knew he was taking a risk and he looked at the situation carefully, but once he decided upon his course of action he was fixed upon it. His joy in his new job is wonderful to see, and a just reward for the time and effort he spent thinking about it.

It may seem as if simply embarking on a spiritual journey is a comparatively small thing and not worth a great deal of consideration. But our spiritual welfare is of an importance above all things, and no such journey should be undertaken lightly. Once embarked upon, we should put our whole heart and soul into ensuring its success.

## Exercise

Find pictures of paths and roads leading into the distance in magazines or on the internet. Make a collage of them and use this as part of your prayer today, asking God for the grace to 'run with perseverance the race that is set before us, looking to Jesus the pioneer and perfecter of our faith' (Hebrews 12:1–2).

# The importance of good companions

I appeal to you, then, be imitators of me. For this reason I sent you Timothy, who is my beloved and faithful child in the Lord, to remind you of my ways in Christ Jesus, as I teach them everywhere in every church. But some of you, thinking that I am not coming to you, have become arrogant.

1 CORINTHIANS 4:16–18

Some time ago, I was discussing with a group of older people the wisdom that they wished they could share with younger generations. They came to the conclusion that the biggest single influence on their lives had been their choice of life partner, and they wanted young people to understand just how important it was to choose wisely in this area. A life partner can influence leisure pursuits and hobbies – going to concerts, for example, although originally equally favoured among other hobbies, may become the main activity of the couple if it is the only interest they both share. One's choice of place to live might be influenced by the location of the partner's family; certainly income and lifestyle will be affected to some degree by the occupation of the partner.

This group looked at wedding preparation courses and events but decided that by the time a couple was ready for this sort of activity it was too late – the partner had already been chosen and the course of life fixed. It was decided instead to hold a course for parents and grandparents of teenagers. This was to enable them to explore opportunities for discussion with young people about life choices and partners, sharing their experiences about the importance of such a decision and the need to not rush into major decisions. They also wanted to discuss the option of not having a life partner, of living a single life in a fulfilled and satisfying manner, rather than always feeling as if a person were missing out. An evening on the way relationships could go wrong and exploring possible solutions, as well as how to end a relationship well, was also included. The course was a success – well attended and energetic, it gave all generations an opportunity to share attitudes to relationships and partners, and everyone benefitted.

In his letter to the church in Corinth, Paul too shares his experience that people in couples, groups or community can have a huge influence on each other, for good or for wrong. That is why Timothy is sent – to be an example for the fledgling community to copy, witnessing his attitude to life and how all parts of his life are influenced by his faith and grounded in worship. The importance of good companions applies to all areas of life, not just personal relationships. Ethical companies, staffed by people who work to high standards of good practice; friends who share common interests and act as mutual support groups; churches filled with people who are committed to God and each other – all have the effect of lifting each individual to a higher plane than they might otherwise achieve, through the knowledge that they are not alone but are supported and encouraged by others.

These companions do not have to be flesh and blood – the characters that fill books, both fiction and non-fiction, can also influence, encourage and support us, offering examples of how to live in situations which are challenging and difficult. For those with limited mobility or many commitments, these companions can be as valuable and precious as those we can see and touch.

## Exercise

You may already have a place in your home where you can write or display encouraging quotations or sayings. If you don't, think about starting one. It can be simply the back of your journal or a separate book dedicated to writing down anything which inspires or encourages you. You can make a display on a noticeboard or in a picture frame – it helps if there is a way that you can add more sayings when you discover them. Include anything you like, Christian or non-Christian, written by a famous person or said by a friend or neighbour. The only criterion should be that it encourages you to continue in the right path as you journey towards contentment.

My only aim is to finish the race and complete the task the Lord Jesus has given me – the task of testifying to the good news of God's grace.
ACTS 20:24 (NIV)

Just keep swimming, swimming, swimming.
Dory from *Finding Nemo* (Walt Disney, 2003)

One more step along the world I go.
Sidney Carter

# Section III

# Finding the rhythm of the way

As we settle into the journey, the energy we have put into our departure lies behind us and different challenges emerge. We have to learn to accept the path, wherever it leads, whether the way is difficult and uneven or smooth-going and fast. We must pace ourselves, pausing to rest and reflect, allowing ourselves time to absorb the insights we have gained, without slipping into inertia and coming to a complete halt. Above all, we must keep moving forwards, not losing sight of the bigger picture among the day-to-day tribulations and delights, trusting always that God travels alongside us and waits patiently for us at our journey's end.

# Stepping aside to pray

**Now during those days he went out to the mountain to pray; and he spent the night in prayer to God.**
LUKE 6:12

For the first few days of going on pilgrimage, the most exacting task is not getting used to the weight of the rucksack or finding the correct route, but finding a rhythm to the journey. Until I have settled into the right rhythm of walking and resting, eating and praying, there is a roughness around the edges of the pilgrimage, a frayed feeling to the walk. It is not until I have become used to the path and know how many hours I can walk before needing a rest, or know when I will stop for prayer and reflection, that I can begin to mesh with the journey. Only then does it begin to give back to me, in insight and wisdom, some of the effort I put into walking and reflecting.

We all know how important it is – to find a rhythm of life which is balanced and sound, to keep the proportions of work and leisure activities sensible so that neither one side nor the other gets a disproportionate number of hours or too much focus. But how difficult it is to make this happen! How easy it is to allow one thing or another to gain too great a significance in our lives, too strong a grip on our attention, forcing other things to fade into the background! And how often it is that those quiet, reflective activities, those things we do which strengthen our hearts and souls but which have no immediate outward benefit, miss out.

The words 'Jesus went out to pray' run like a golden thread through the gospels: 'he went up the mountain by himself to pray' (Matthew 14:23); 'he threw himself on the ground and prayed' (Matthew 26:39); 'he got up and went out to a deserted place, and there he prayed' (Mark 1:35); 'he was praying in a certain place' (Luke 11:1); 'he withdrew again to the mountain by himself' (John 6:15). At intervals throughout his journey through towns and villages, between visits to temples and houses, Jesus would withdraw from the crowd, even from his disciples, and find a place to be alone. There, he would strengthen his connection to God, deepen his relationship, find once again the strength, wisdom and love to continue in his task. It wasn't always easy, even for Jesus – too often the demands of the crowd would follow him; sometimes even his disciples tried to prevent him from finding time apart. But he calmly and firmly set all these calls upon his time aside until he had prayed, knowing that it was only through these times of quiet, of connection, that he would be able to deal with the other times of clamour and noise.

So too with us. It might be that our lives are very well structured, that there is a pattern to our days which allows for planning. In this case, it should be comparatively simple to work out the best time to allocate to prayer and reflection, reading and reflection. Most people find it easiest to use the same time each day, even the same place, so that the pull of the familiar increases over time and helps us in our efforts to find time to be aware of God's presence. For others, the season of their lives will not allow for this type of timetabled interaction – then it can be a case of simply determining that before the end of each day a certain amount of time will be spent in quiet, with God. But for all of us, the truth remains the same: we will not have the strength to carry out God's work if we are not first connected to God, the strength of the vine, of which we are only branches and whose fruit we bear.

> To be a Christian without prayer is no more possible than to be alive without breathing.
> Martin Luther

## Exercise

Try creating a 'wilderness space' – a room or a corner of a room, or even just a chair with a table next to it, for journal, Bible, pens and prompts for prayer. If you pause and pray every time you pass that area, then the habit of prayer will be developed and it will become easier to keep to a regular time of reflection and prayer.

# Taking time to rest

**For thus said the Lord God, the Holy One of Israel: In returning and rest you shall be saved; in quietness and in trust shall be your strength.**
ISAIAH 30:15

One of the most important things to factor in when planning a long pilgrimage on foot is the notion of rest days. It is possible to walk a large number of miles per day for days on end, but there comes a time when the human body can do this no longer and has to stop to recover and rebuild. For 21st-century pilgrims, who have perhaps been leading a fairly sedentary life previously, this time can come quite soon – blistered feet or strained leg muscles can benefit from a break from walking after only five or six days. In other cases, a break every ten days or so of walking will enable muscles to recover – and small administrative tasks, such as cleaning kit and repairing breakages, to take place.

This may seem like shirking the task, and there will undoubtedly be other pilgrims who walk on, making the one who rests feel very weak and a bit pathetic. However, each pilgrim must listen to the demands of their own body, rather than give in to the pressure of others who may be more experienced walkers – or simply unaware of the dangers of pushing themselves too hard. The risk involved in not resting when injured or weary is that the blisters or the strain will become progressively worse and will finally endanger the whole journey, threatening the walker's ability to finish. I have met people weeping with frustration as they have been forced to cut short their journey of a lifetime, due to aggressive blisters or pulled muscles. All the planning and preparation, the cost and the effort, come to nothing for the sake of a few days' rest or at least a few days of less mileage.

The same is true of our spiritual lives. We can drift away from God and spend time in anxious planning or worrying. We can even find ourselves becoming weary simply from the effort of following a new and unfamiliar spiritual routine. Then we need to remember that it is in God that we will find the rest and quietness we seek, and take some time simply to rest in him. This can be done on a daily basis by bringing our minds back to God's love for us at frequent intervals during the day. We can pause and say a particular Bible verse which brings comfort and peace, perhaps, or say a short 'arrow' prayer which calls on God to make his presence felt to us. As well as this, at regular intervals, it is good to set aside a block of time – a day is ideal, an hour is fine if you do not have a day – simply to enjoy God's presence.

Rest gives strength. Rest reminds us that God is in control and that all we need to do is trust in him and he will lead us on the correct path, sharing our burdens and straightening the road before us.

# Exercise

Try to incorporate a pattern of rest into your daily or weekly spiritual routine. Take some time out from your day – or even a whole day if possible – and enter consciously into the presence of God. You can do this by spending time in prayer and meditation if this comes easily to you. However, it may be that this is too challenging, and you need a rest from effortful prayer or conscious striving to be aware of God. In this case, rest can be found in different ways. You could read a good book, such as a classic of theology or a favourite devotional; try one of C.S. Lewis' theology books, or 'The Chronicles of Narnia' series, if you want something light, or ask at your nearest Christian bookshop for recommendations. If you prefer, you can take a walk in the countryside or a park, enjoying the evidence of God's goodness in creation. You could prepare your favourite meal, and take time to enjoy the richness and variety of the flavours of food. Or you could listen to a piece of music, and thank God for the sounds and harmonies which you can hear. Spend time in a way which reminds you of God's love for you and all creation, so that you can re-enter your daily life refreshed and renewed in your confidence and trust in God.

# Remember the long way

**This entire commandment that I command you today you must diligently observe, so that you may live and increase, and go in and occupy the land that the Lord promised on oath to your ancestors. Remember the long way that the Lord your God has led you these forty years in the wilderness, in order to humble you, testing you to know what was in your heart, whether or not you would keep his commandments. He humbled you by letting you hunger, then by feeding you with manna, with which neither you nor your ancestors were acquainted, in order to make you understand that one does not live by bread alone, but by every word that comes from the mouth of the Lord.**

DEUTERONOMY 8:1–3

As a parish priest, I have spent many hours by the bedsides of the elderly and sick. Sometimes I have prayed with them; at other times, all that was needed was a friendly face, someone to talk to who could fend off the fears of loneliness and old age. I have heard the life stories of all sorts of people, of every character and type. I have listened to the experiences of people who were once administrators of large parts of foreign countries, enjoying almost unimaginable wealth and privilege, and heard tales of village life from those for whom a trip to the nearest town was an occasional event and to the nearest city an annual celebration. Their memories, though, are curiously similar – common to both is the importance and value of people they have known and loved. Marriages, births, deaths, friends, relatives – anecdotes about children, spouses, friends are told again and again, as if the teller was picking up an old and much-loved object and looking at it once more, holding it in their hands and treasuring it.

But alongside these deep-seated and precious memories, there will often run a sense of surprise – and gratitude – for the way life has turned out. I will hear of unexpected incidents that changed the course of a lifetime – a meeting missed, perhaps, or a chance encounter with an old acquaintance. These incidents stand out like pearls on a necklace, the thread of everyday life and happenings joining bright, surprising events and occasions which remain memorable when much of the normal things of life have dimmed. The storyteller will often muse that although it did not seem like it at the time, such an event or such a meeting changed the course of their life, and if they are Christian, they might well remark that God was, after all, looking after them all this time!

The writer of Deuteronomy 8 is writing the words of Moses, and he has a task to perform: he must remind his audience that the goodness of God should not be forgotten in times of well-being and prosperity. They should not allow their desperate and terrifying escape from Egypt and subsequent wanderings in the desert to fade away in the face of current wealth and self-satisfaction. The writer recalls for their benefit the way that God cared for them throughout this time, as they wandered and struggled, but he reminds them of something more: all their hardships and sufferings were for their own good, training in character and purpose, so that the children of Israel would always remember to rely first on God, whatever the circumstances.

The journey towards contentment might well be a difficult one – it will almost certainly bring surprises. We must not expect our spiritual lives to progress smoothly and in carefully graded steps, but instead we must accept the uncertainty of the journey, embracing those times of insecurity and anxiety about the future, finding in them a means of growing in faith and hope.

## Exercise

On a large piece of paper, draw a string of beads – large circles or ovals joined by a single thread. Along the thread sections, write all those daily activities and meetings which bring you joy or in which you find satisfaction. In the beads, write or draw those events in your life which have been unexpected but which altered the course of your life. These may be a chance meeting which has led to a new job or hobby or an unexpected event. They might not always be happy things – an accident, an illness or the loss of a friend or partner, perhaps. For these, try to draw out the lessons learnt and the way your character has been shaped and strengthened.

When you have finished, ask God for the grace 'to walk in all his ways, to love him, to serve the Lord your God with all your heart and with all your soul' (Deuteronomy 10:12).

# Run with perseverance

Therefore, since we are surrounded by so great a cloud of witnesses, let us also lay aside every weight and the sin that clings so closely, and let us run with perseverance the race that is set before us, looking to Jesus the pioneer and perfecter of our faith, who for the sake of the joy that was set before him endured the cross, disregarding its shame, and has taken his seat at the right hand of the throne of God.

HEBREWS 12:1–2

Most of us have experienced what it is like to run a race – even if that experience now resides in the distant past. We can go back in our minds and sort through childhood memories of sports days, with their accompanying triumph or disaster; athletics lessons at schools, those chalky white lines marking out running tracks of various distances; or simply running for the sheer joy of it, through streets or meadows, parks or fields. Whatever sort of running we did, the elements remain the same. First, there is the decision even before the race to run as fast as we can in an effort to win it or at least not to come too far behind the rest. Then there is the vast amount of energy required to keep us moving at the fastest speed we can manage. This energy is fuelled by our determination not to slow down or stop, even when we are becoming tired and the effort is growing greater. Finally, there is the sight of the finish line, which we fix our eyes upon, watching as it grows ever closer.

This wonderful, famous passage from Hebrews contains all the elements of running a race, comparing it to living the Christian life.

The writer reminds us that to be a Christian is not an easy option, that it involves effort and energy. We are told that we must not cease our effort but must fix our eyes on that wonderful finishing line, which is a perfect relationship with Christ. This sounds like very hard work, and it is understandable that we might, on reading this passage, feel that Christianity is a very challenging way of life. But we can be heartened by many things within this passage. As every runner knows, the more running we do, the easier it gets. Muscles get stronger and faster; they recover more quickly from the effort, building resistance and gaining speed. The body gets more used to the effort and the race becomes easier, with speeds increasing.

So too with practising the faith – we can lay down the weight of regret for past actions in the knowledge that we have been forgiven of our sins, making the journey easier and faster. As we continue to practise spiritual exercises, we will develop our 'prayer muscles', so that they become flexible and strong. We have the example before us of the greatest athlete of all, Christ himself, who is not only the goal of the race, but is also our running companion, urging us on for his sake and for our own. And all the time, the race is being run in the company of a crowd of supporters, a 'cloud of witnesses' who are cheering us on, willing us to reach the finish line.

# Exercise

Find pictures of athletes and runners, of racetracks and finish lines. Decorate your prayer space with these, to remind yourself of the race you are running.

If you prefer words, find some motivational quotes to display or write in your journal. For example:

> We all have dreams. In order to make dreams come into reality it takes an awful lot of determination, dedication, self-discipline and effort.
> Jesse Owens

> Don't stop when you are tired; stop when you are done.
> Marilyn Monroe

> Running is the greatest metaphor for life, because you get out of it what you put into it.
> Oprah Winfrey

> Some sessions are stars and some are stones, but in the end they are all rocks and we build upon them.
> Chrissie Wellington

If you are the sort of person who is encouraged by rewards, design yourself a set of medals, to be awarded to yourself for your spiritual progress. This can be for remembering to take time to pray each day, completing a particular book or study, or trying to adopt a certain attitude towards something or someone you find challenging.

**15**

# Trusting in God

Then Jesus told them a parable about their need to pray always and not to lose heart. He said, 'In a certain city there was a judge who neither feared God nor had respect for people. In that city there was a widow who kept coming to him and saying, "Grant me justice against my opponent." For a while he refused; but later he said to himself, "Though I have no fear of God and no respect for anyone, yet because this widow keeps bothering me, I will grant her justice, so that she may not wear me out by continually coming."' And the Lord said, 'Listen to what the unjust judge says. And will not God grant justice to his chosen ones who cry to him day and night? Will he delay long in helping them? I tell you, he will quickly grant justice to them.'

LUKE 18:1–8

This is not the sort of parable we are used to encountering, for this is not a direct comparison between God and the unjust judge. How could that be, since this judge has no fear of God and no respect for anyone. This judge disregards the pleas of a widow, one for whom special regard is commanded by the Torah, one to whom the community owes particular care. This story is more of a stepping stone – a way of moving from something small to something greater. That is, we are led to reflect on the way that, just as someone as callous and hard as the judge finally answers the widow's request, so God, who has infinite love for all of his creation, will much more readily answer our prayers.

How comforting this must have been to the people Luke was addressing, those beleaguered early Christians, who had been waiting patiently and expectantly through persecution and hardship for the second coming of Christ, which they had been confidently told was imminent and for which they waited so hopefully. 'Pray always,' they are told, 'don't lose heart.' It must have been hard to sustain a level of alertness and readiness for something which was so long in coming, and Luke offers words of reassurance and hope.

Those words apply still to us, so many generations later, who are still waiting and hoping, still praying without ceasing. It can be so hard to keep praying, offering heartfelt intercessions for change, justice, healing, for ourselves or for those we love. It can take so much effort daily to wrestle again in prayer, asking in hope and confidence for that same gift or miracle when it seems that the only answer is silence. But we must continue, we must not lose heart, for our prayers will be answered – in God's time. And in the meantime we wait, and in the waiting we are changed. Prayer changes us as we wait and hope. We become more aware of the needs of others, more aware of the presence of God, more aware of God, even in the silence of unanswered prayer. As the theologian Frederick Buechner wrote, we must continue to pray 'not because you have to beat a path to God's door before [God will] open it, but because until you beat the path, maybe there's no way of getting to your door' (*Wishful Thinking*, 1973).

So today, as every day, let us faithfully pray, let us hold before God the needs of the world and of our deepest selves, confident that our prayers will be answered, hopeful that in the praying we will ourselves be transformed, so that when there is a knock on the door, we will hear it and answer. 'For everyone who asks receives, and everyone who searches finds, and for everyone who knocks, the door will be opened' (Luke 11:10).

## Exercise

If you do not already do so, consider keeping a prayer journal. In this, you can keep a record not only of the people and causes you are praying for, but, more importantly, of answered prayer. Too often, when our prayers are answered, there is a moment of rejoicing and affirmation which is all too soon forgotten as we move on to the next request, the next heartfelt plea. If we write down not only the prayer but also the way in which it was answered and when, including also our reactions to this answered prayer, we have a permanent reminder of God's faithfulness to us. It will provide support and comfort when it seems that God is silent, a book of hope for the dark days and reassurance for when the work of prayer appears fruitless.

I pray because I can't help myself. I pray because I'm helpless.
I pray because the need flows out of me all the time, waking and sleeping. It doesn't change God. It changes me.

C.S. Lewis in *Shadowlands* by William Nicholson

# Section IV

## The dangers of discontent

Discontent is like the snake in the garden of Eden – often present just below our consciousness, always ready with unhappy comparisons, envious reflections, covetous comments which slide into our minds, making us unhappy with our lot, encouraging us to scorn that which we have and envy the perceived achievements, acquisitions or status of others. The power of rationalising these thoughts and feelings is strong, and it takes much effort to withstand them. But we must arm ourselves against this sly discontent and journey on bravely and energetically, not measuring ourselves against other frail mortals, but striving always to become more like Christ – our ultimate role model.

# This teaching is difficult

'I am the bread of life. Your ancestors ate the manna in the wilderness, and they died. This is the bread that comes down from heaven, so that one may eat of it and not die. I am the living bread that came down from heaven. Whoever eats of this bread will live forever; and the bread that I will give for the life of the world is my flesh'... When many of his disciples heard it, they said, 'This teaching is difficult; who can accept it?'

JOHN 6:48–51, 60

I once attended a conference for clergy on servant leadership – an exploration of the way in which parish priests could be better leaders by being the servants of the communities they led. The philosophy was that by turning the power pyramid upside down, the leader's role became that of a servant, putting the needs of others first and enabling all to reach their full potential. The course was interesting and well led, but there were some minor administrative issues which led to confusion over meals and some room allocations. At the end of the course, we gathered in our small groups one last time to assess how the weekend had gone. To begin with, the discussion went well – we talked about some of the things we had learnt and the suggestions we had heard. Then an older priest joined in. Throughout the entire weekend, he had been a dissonant voice – disagreeing with the staff, complaining about the meal arrangements, questioning the conclusions of the teaching. Now he started in with a litany of complaints, piling one on top of the other. The rest of the group began to join in, encouraged to pick up on small things which had not gone well and articulate them to everyone else. In a very short time, the group went from being essentially satisfied and happy to being angry and discontented. The group's feedback was negative and hostile, which in turn affected the rest of the conference delegates as well as the teaching staff. Reflecting on this, I was astonished at how easily the group had changed from being one that was essentially supportive and happy to one that was restless and complaining – and all under the influence of just one member.

Jesus also suffered from the effects of complaints and grumbling. In the passage above, it is his disciples who wish to turn from teaching which is too challenging for them. Much of their time with Jesus is spent trying to understand the words of his which turn traditional thinking upside down – those who want to be first will be last; to enter the rule of God, one must become like a little child; nothing is hidden except to become known; whoever wants to save one's life must lose it. Beyond the circle of supporters, Jesus has others who grumble and complain against him, and it is these people who eventually win the day, dreaming up false charges and having him put to death.

The effect of complaining and grumbling should not be under-estimated – it has the power to undermine the greatest of initiatives, to bring down to earth the most exciting of dreams, to destroy the best of visions. As Christians, we know what it is like to live in hope, and we accept the discipline of doing so. Murmurs and complaints, however gentle they may seem, however quiet the undertone in which they are muttered, undermine and eventually destroy. Far better to focus on the good which you can perceive, however slight this may be. Good things rarely emerge from people's complaints; these simply weigh others down, causing them to focus on the faults, not the virtues, of an action or event. Praising someone's efforts in some small way, focusing on the good which has been achieved, builds people up and encourages them to try harder and, hopefully, to achieve the end for which they originally aimed.

## Exercise

Spend today reflecting on the words you speak about others' actions. Are they encouraging or dismissive? Notice the occasions when you complain about something – do you do this often or rarely? Is what you say helpful or critical? Notice even the slightest criticism – about the length of a queue in a shop, for example. How does this help matters? What could you say instead? Try to anticipate your criticisms and complaints and substitute instead some words of support or praise. This will be difficult and seem clumsy to begin with, but you will soon form the habit of encouragement.

A word of encouragement during failure is worth more than an hour of praise after success.

Anonymous

# Martha was distracted

> Now as they went on their way, he entered a certain village, where a woman named Martha welcomed him into her home. She had a sister named Mary, who sat at the Lord's feet and listened to what he was saying. But Martha was distracted by her many tasks; so she came to him and asked, 'Lord, do you not care that my sister has left me to do all the work by myself? Tell her then to help me.' But the Lord answered her, 'Martha, Martha, you are worried and distracted by many things; there is need of only one thing. Mary has chosen the better part, which will not be taken away from her.'
>
> LUKE 10:38–42

Poor Martha! Time and again in sermons and books, lectures and articles, she is held up as the exemplar of the dangers of busyness, of being so distracted by the everyday little things that we forget the most important things and of being overburdened by 'doing' to the exclusion of 'being'. And this is indeed the case – Martha is chided by Jesus for being 'worried and distracted by many things', for focusing on the ephemeral and the workaday, while her sister looks instead to the kingdom and seeks to make the most of the precious time she has with Jesus. It is a valuable lesson for us, once again, to remember to make sure of our priorities and not allow the small things to crowd out the important or significant things.

But Martha, we might think to ourselves, is only playing the part of a good hostess. She is offering hospitality to a much-loved visitor, ensuring his comfort. This too is true, and offering generous hospitality to guests is an important part of our lives as Christians – welcoming people into our homes and churches, making them feel included as part of our community. But the manner in which Martha carries out her tasks does not set such a good example. She is not only worried and distracted in herself, but comes and disturbs Jesus and Mary, offering complaints against Mary and urging Jesus to make her get up and help.

Part of the task of learning contentment is finding satisfaction in the everyday, the normal routine of things, even those tedious jobs which we might dislike and be tempted to despise. Instead of fretting about them and complaining about the necessity of carrying them out, how much better to seek the good in whatever we do, however mundane it might seem. In this, we would be following the example of Brother Lawrence, a 17th-century French monk who began work in the monastery in the lowliest position – scrubbing vegetables, washing dishes, sweeping the floor. Instead of complaining about these tasks and resenting the amount of time they took, time which could otherwise be spent in prayer and worship, Brother Lawrence decided to make his work his worship, writing: 'Is it not quicker and easier just to do our common business wholly for the love of him?' In this way, even the humblest task becomes an act of worship and gains great value through that. As Brother Lawrence noted: 'It is enough for me to pick up but a straw from the ground for the love of God.'

# Exercise

It might be too much to expect ourselves not to complain or feel some resentment at the tedium of some of the tasks we carry out each day, but if we begin in a small way, we will soon train our minds to find contentment in everything we do. During your prayer time or the time you set aside for reflection, think of one task or job you do every day or frequently which you find tedious but necessary. It might be clearing up after other people, performing household tasks or a routine job at work. Resolve that each day you will perform this task without fretting or grumbling about it, neither openly in front of other people nor in your own mind. Instead, you will carry it out with joy and dedication, as if it were the most interesting and rewarding thing you will do all day. See what a difference this attitude makes to the way you approach the task and the effect it has on others around you. Write or draw your reactions – do they change and develop as you continue in this attitude? Try to sustain this for a number of days – does it become a habit?

*A servant with this clause*
*Makes drudgery divine:*
*Who sweeps a room as for Thy laws,*
*Makes that and th' action fine.*

*This is the famous stone*
*That turneth all to gold;*
*For that which God doth touch and own*
*Cannot for less be told.*

George Herbert, 'The Elixir' (1633)

# Angry enough to die

**The Lord God appointed a bush, and made it come up over Jonah, to give shade over his head, to save him from his discomfort; so Jonah was very happy about the bush. But when dawn came up the next day, God appointed a worm that attacked the bush, so that it withered. When the sun rose, God prepared a sultry east wind, and the sun beat down on the head of Jonah so that he was faint and asked that he might die. He said, 'It is better for me to die than to live.'**

**But God said to Jonah, 'Is it right for you to be angry about the bush?' And he said, 'Yes, angry enough to die.' Then the Lord said, 'You are concerned about the bush, for which you did not labour and which you did not grow; it came into being in a night and perished in a night. And should I not be concerned about Nineveh, that great city, in which there are more than a hundred and twenty thousand people who do not know their right hand from their left, and also many animals?'**

JONAH 4:6–11

People become angry over many things – when they see injustice to others or themselves, when they have been hurt or frightened, when they or those they love are threatened and they feel unsafe. Anger slides beneath the barriers we construct against it when we are hungry or tired, stressed or frustrated. This sort of anger can flare up suddenly and spend itself in one great outburst, or it can simmer away for a while, slowly becoming hotter until the person reaches 'boiling point' and explodes in violent or bitter words or actions. This sort of anger is regretted almost immediately after it has expressed itself. It can cause hurt and fear or provoke anger in return, thus beginning a destructive cycle of violent words or actions. It is this sort of anger that God encounters in Jonah – and for which he gently chides him. Jonah's anger at the death of the bush is shown to be childish and irrational. God uses the situation to show not only that Jonah's anger is wrong in itself but also that the anger Jonah wishes God to show is equally wrong. The greater the hurt, God seems to be saying, the greater the need for forgiveness and reconciling action rather than retaliation.

We all get angry – sometimes with justification and other times when a more measured response might be better. Anger can be a destructive, corrosive emotion, which is rarely productive of good results. Even if the cause is just, surely it is better to change the anger we feel to a desire to remedy wrongs through positive action, rather than to wield it against someone. Anger can cloud our judgement and alter our perception of the way things are. It can be a barrier between us and God. It can certainly be a barrier between us and the contentment we seek. How can we see the right path, the just approach, and how can we determine which reconciling words to use, which actions to take to remedy wrongs, if our emotions are in turmoil and our mood is hot with rage? Not for nothing are we urged to refrain from anger: 'One who is slow to anger is better than the mighty, and one whose temper is controlled than one who captures a city' (Proverbs 16:32).

## Exercise

When you are angry today, pause and take note. Try to step back from your anger, to observe what you are feeling in a detached manner rather than becoming deeply engaged with it. Notice what it was that made you angry – was it justifiable or not? Why did you become angry? Was it on your behalf or that of somebody else? What other emotion might you have felt? Were your feelings aggravated by your tiredness or stress? Very often, simply the act of stepping back and reflecting will dissipate your anger.

If you continue to be angry, remember how you feel, and write or draw the causes of your anger and your reactions. Ask God for insight as to how you might have acted differently.

Refrain from anger, and forsake wrath. Do not fret – it leads only to evil.
PSALM 37:8

# The way of the lazy

**The way of the lazy is overgrown with thorns, but the path of the upright is a level highway.**
PROVERBS 15:19

Throughout the Old Testament there appear a group of stories with the same theme – exploring what happens to those who do not wish to go to the trouble or effort of trusting God, those who do not 'wait upon the Lord', but try to arrange things to their benefit in their own way. Saul, after the death of Samuel the prophet, goes to visit the witch of Endor to find out his future (1 Samuel 28:3–19); King Asa forges an alliance with the king of Aram, rather than trust in God to deliver him from his enemies (2 Chronicles 16:1–10); more famously, Jacob does not wait for Isaac's blessing but cheats his brother out of it, in his hurry to speed his future (Genesis 27). Similarly, Jonah tried to avoid his mission to Nineveh, because he feared the subsequent repercussions (Jonah 1), and Balaam had to be physically restrained by his donkey from giving in to the officials of Balak (Numbers 22:21–39).

Some of these stories are better known than others, but they carry a cumulative message of warning to those who try to take a particular approach. And what is this approach? It can be seen as a type of laziness, a desire to avoid the effort involved in trusting in God, a reluctance to place one's future in God's hand, but instead looking to an easier path, one where the control stays within our grasp and where we feel we can be in charge of our destiny instead of God. It never ends well, this path: 'For the eyes of the Lord range throughout the entire earth, to strengthen those whose heart is true to him. You have done foolishly in this; for from now on you will have wars' (2 Chronicles 16:9). Too often that route which we thought would achieve our ends the quickest is shown to be strewn with thorns and obstructions. If we had only trusted in God and waited on his time, rather than trying to rush things through in ours, we would have avoided much pain and trouble.

'The way of the lazy is overgrown with thorns' – the path to God's side, the path of prayer and reflection, of listening and patience, quickly shows the effect of neglect. And the longer we leave it, the harder it is to walk along it. Notice how the path is not overgrown merely with weeds, according to the writer of the Proverbs, but sharp thorns, which tear fabric and scratch at the flesh. In contrast, once the path is well used, it becomes gradually easier to use, until even the ups and downs of the emotional landscape are levelled out and the one seeking God has a smooth path.

Praying every day is not always easy. We may become overburdened with things to do or a domestic or work crisis may take up all our time, leaving none for anything else. We may lose heart, fearing that our deepest desires and requests will never be granted by a God who apparently isn't listening. Or we may grow lazy, tired of doing the work of prayer, especially when it seems to bring no good. God works in his time, but he always works; we must simply continue in prayer, not seeking shortcuts or to carry out the tasks in our own strength, but trusting in the creator God.

## Exercise

Review your prayer time. Are the physical conditions still helpful? Do you need to change the time of day when you pray because other circumstances in your life have changed? Do you need to change the location of your prayer corner or prayer space? Do you use books of prayers or reflections to help you? Should you? If you do, do you find them useful or should you change them? Is the way you pray the most beneficial for you? Should there be more quiet or more reading? Would music make a difference? Try a different prayer style, or go more deeply into the one that you use already. Don't forget to journal – it is the greatest way to see God's answer to prayer in God's own way and in his own time!

# Section V

# The path of contentment: living lightly

We have now become used to the way – our prayer practices should sit more easily with us, as the period we have set aside for reflection becomes part of our daily timetable and our habits of prayer are beginning to be formed.

Now is the time to move deeper in our exploration of contentment, looking at some of the principles which lie behind contented Christian life and trying to incorporate them further into our lives. We become more serious in our efforts to rid ourselves of distraction in the form of material possessions, acknowledging that these preoccupy us and weigh us down both mentally and physically. We turn our focus away from the power and influence of this world and look for ways of living in the next. We begin to practise seriously the way of Christian generosity, giving freely of our time, love and money to those who have need of it, both within our community and beyond.

# Aliens and exiles

Beloved, I urge you as aliens and exiles to abstain from the desires of the flesh that wage war against the soul. Conduct yourselves honourably among the Gentiles, so that, though they malign you as evildoers, they may see your honourable deeds and glorify God when he comes to judge.

1 PETER 2:11–12

I can't help it – whenever I hear the word 'alien', my mind goes directly to small creatures from outer space, usually green in colour. These creatures are more often than not perfectly friendly and wish the planet no harm, having landed here in their spaceships quite by accident and with no other desire than to get their ship fixed and go home.

Or my mind will move to those fearful camps set up in our country-side during World War II to house 'enemy aliens': people who had perhaps spent many years in this country – to all intents ordinary citizens – but who now found themselves, by virtue of the fact that their country of origin was now at war with ours, classed as 'the enemy' and treated accordingly.

I tend to be more traditional in my reflections on the word 'exile', calling to mind the children of Israel as they spent years in Babylon. As a conquered people sent away from the land promised to them by God, they spent their time in mourning for what had passed and in longing for a return to their homeland.

Although Peter writes neither of green men nor victims of war, he does mean those who are displaced, and both 'aliens' and 'exiles' contain overtones of sadness and longing – a feeling of being where one shouldn't, of having the challenges of living and growing made greater by the fact that they must be undertaken in a place which is not of one's choosing.

So why does Peter, in his letter to the faithful, urge us to live as 'aliens and exiles'? Why would we willingly put ourselves among the displaced, the excluded, the disadvantaged? Because, contradictory as it may seem, it is when we are at our most comfortable that we are least likely to grow and change. It is often when everything is going right for us, when life is easy, that we slow down on our spiritual journey.

It seems strange that a journey to contentment can be hampered by physical, mental and spiritual ease and stability, but too often that stability can degenerate into stagnation, that ease can become mere passivity. Then we are in danger of becoming too attached to those places, situations and relationships that trouble us the least – the undemanding, the ones with no risk, no danger of having our minds shaken or awakened to new thoughts. For the Christian, the awareness that this earth is not our final resting place must be always present; we must not become so entranced by the things of this world that we begin to collude with the status quo. By remembering that we too are aliens and exiles, we align ourselves with all those who suffer the same fate – willingly or unwillingly. We can reach out in empathy and love, sharing their vulnerability and working for our return to 'home', wherever that is.

## Exercise

Reflect on the two words 'alien' and 'exile'. What pictures first come into your mind? Bring these words to apply to your own situation. Are there occasions when you have felt like an alien or exile? How did it feel to be in that position? What did you learn from that experience and how has it changed you? How can you bring this into your prayer life?

You might wish to make a collage of pictures from magazines or the internet of what the words mean to you. If you search for 'alien', you will inevitably get some strange pictures, but they might help as a picture of inner strangeness, of not belonging. Searching for 'living in exile' will bring all sorts of pictures – springboards for reflection.

# Foxes have holes

As they were going along the road, someone said to him, 'I will follow you wherever you go.' And Jesus said to him, 'Foxes have holes, and birds of the air have nests; but the Son of Man has nowhere to lay his head.'

LUKE 9:57–58

It is interesting how Jesus calls his disciples. To some, such as Peter and Andrew, it is necessary to say only, 'Follow me,' and they do, leaving behind everything, the entire make-up of their lives to that point, simply to follow Jesus. Others require more convincing – Philip gets Nathanael and tells him he has seen the Messiah. Nathanael's doubt – 'Can anything good come out of Nazareth?' – is overcome by Jesus' knowledge of him, even down to where he has been: 'I saw you under the fig tree' (John 1:46, 48). With other followers, however, it seems that Jesus looks into their hearts and can tell what the obstacles will be to following him and how great that person will discover them to be. Some people cannot overcome these obstacles, which they themselves have placed in the path of their discipleship – the rich young man finds himself unable to 'sell your possessions, and give the money to the poor' and goes away 'grieving, for he had many possessions' (Matthew 19:21–22).

We do not know what happens to the man in our passage today who would follow Jesus, but he is warned that this may mean he will have to give up all notions of place and home. Jesus has 'set his face to go to Jerusalem' (Luke 9:51), so is on his way there, journeying from Mount Tabor, site of the transfiguration, through the countryside to the city of his death. He is approached by a man who has presumably heard of the miracles of Jesus or perhaps witnessed them himself. Or he may have been present on the hillside when Jesus preached or shared the meal that was enough to feed 5,000 people. Whatever the reason, this man wants to follow Jesus, but Jesus looks into his heart and tells him the words which presumably will deter him the most: 'Do you realise that you will be able to call no place home if you decide to follow me?'

Following Jesus is a journey which requires wholehearted commitment. Those of us who set out along this journey cannot hold anything back – certainly we cannot hope to stay in the same place. We must be prepared to endure discomforts and inconveniences, all the trials and little annoyances we encounter whenever we leave the safe routine of our everyday lives. We must live to another timetable, one that is not arranged solely for our benefit. We may find comfortable resting places along the way – places of spiritual delight and emotional satisfaction – but we must be prepared to leave these behind as we journey on, forever making new discoveries and facing new challenges.

However, although the challenges might be great, we can be sure that not only is Jesus our journey companion, but that we can find a home in his loving care for each one of us, a home which fulfils all our requirements and in which we will find a comfort and ease which we will not experience anywhere else.

# Exercise

What does 'home' mean to you? It is a very laden word, carrying many different meanings – to every person it will mean something unique, composed of past experience and future hope.

Consider the place where you live at the moment – is it where you hope to remain or are you searching for somewhere else? How would you feel if you had to leave it all behind tomorrow? What would you miss the most? What would you do if you were put in the same position as the man in Luke?

Now consider the other things which make a home for you – being known in your community, perhaps, or the work you do. Does home include the people with whom you share the place you live? How might you feel if you were asked to give all this up as well? How present does Jesus feel in your home? What could you do to welcome him in? Physical indications such as prayer spaces, pictures or words can help change an atmosphere – how might you use these in your home?

# Where your treasure is

'Do not store up for yourselves treasures on earth, where moth and rust consume and where thieves break in and steal; but store up for yourselves treasures in heaven, where neither moth nor rust consumes and where thieves do not break in and steal. For where your treasure is, there your heart will be also.'

MATTHEW 6:19–21

What a challenging statement this is from Jesus – part of a lengthy exploration of what it means to live a Christ-focused life. Following on from those glorious, radical, life-giving statements of blessing which begin the sermon on the mount, Jesus proceeds to tell his listeners how they can live out these injunctions in a way which gives glory to God. We are told to make peace with those with whom we have a grievance, to live restrained personal lives, not seeking physical gratification if it comes at the cost of personal integrity or harm to another. We are enjoined to love our enemies and pray for them, to give generously, to pray and – here – not to store up treasures for ourselves.

We are told that the material goods of the world are liable to get lost or broken, that they are impermanent and will ultimately do us no good. I hope that you have already proceeded quite a long way along the path of living light to material goods and possessions (see 'Nothing for the journey' on page 30). Perhaps you have discovered a lightening of the heart and mind as you have rid yourself of unnecessary objects, clearing your home of things which bring no joy or serve no purpose except to cause anxiety for their security and greed for further acquisitions. If you have, then congratulations! If you are finding the exercise a struggle, do not lose heart. The journey to contentment is not an easy path, but will become more navigable if it is not littered with the obstacles of material goods and possessions for you to clamber over or step around.

However, this is only the first part of the story, for Jesus does not merely remind us not to store up treasures on earth; he also tells us to store up treasures in heaven. What might these be? They certainly aren't anything physical, as that is an impossibility. The answer is probably as personal as each individual, but suggestions can be found in the text surrounding this one. Every time we pray for our enemies, we store up treasure in heaven (Matthew 5:44); every time we give generously to those who ask (Matthew 5:42), resolve disputes with those with whom we share our lives (Matthew 5:24) or refuse to allow ourselves to be tempted by things which, although harmful, still attract us (Matthew 5:28); every time we refuse to allow ourselves to become anxious over things we cannot control but instead place our trust in God (Matthew 6:25), then we store up treasures in heaven. Praying regularly, sharing the life of our church community, living peacefully with those around us – all these actions drop like golden coins into a metaphorical heavenly treasure chest. And just as the heart of the rich man is filled with joy at the sign of his growing hoard of treasure, so our hearts will rejoice as they become more firmly fixed on the things of God. 'For where your treasure is, there your heart will be also.'

## Exercise

Make your own heavenly treasure chest. Either decorate a box to look like a treasure chest or find a money box or similar container. Encourage yourself by adding to your treasure chest every time you pray, resist temptation or successfully solve a dispute or argument. If this is too difficult to maintain, try adding to your collection when you take up a new service within your church or community, or undertake something on behalf of another. Your treasure can be anything you like – buttons, paperclips, Post-it notes. Or you can use real money, which has the advantage of enabling you to act generously too, as when your chest or container is full, the contents can be given away.

If making a treasure chest is not possible, try drawing one in your journal or on a large piece of paper. Round the outside, write or draw some of the things you can do which will fill your chest. Don't forget cultivating attitudes of mind, such as patience, forbearance, optimism and trust.

# Whose will those things be?

Then he told them a parable: 'The land of a rich man produced abundantly. And he thought to himself, "What should I do, for I have no place to store my crops?" Then he said, "I will do this: I will pull down my barns and build larger ones, and there I will store all my grain and my goods. And I will say to my soul, Soul, you have ample goods laid up for many years; relax, eat, drink, be merry." But God said to him, "You fool! This very night your life is being demanded of you. And the things you have prepared, whose will they be?" So it is with those who store up treasures for themselves but are not rich towards God.'

LUKE 12:16–21

I recently had the privilege of undertaking a tour of the Holy Land with a group of clergy. It was a familiarisation tour, designed to introduce us to this wonderful country and its heritage so that we in turn could guide others. We hurtled from site to site at breath-taking speed, so it was not until the end of the trip that we could reflect on all that we had seen and done and give thanks for such an opportunity. One of the joys of the trip was meeting a group of people engaged in ministry. Drawn from all over the UK, with some from the USA as well, we spent long hours in each other's company – and delightful company it was too. Away from the responsibility of the working environment, each person could relax and share experiences. This indeed was a joy, as too often relationships are entangled and corrupted by the strings of power, authority, responsibility and judgement, which wrap around us and prevent us from seeing clearly and valuing accordingly.

We were lucky on that trip, as no one was too caught up in the delights of power and privilege or felt the need to remind everyone constantly of their importance and dignity. I have been at other gatherings, of all sorts, where this has not been the case. Conversations with people who are constantly looking over your shoulders to find someone more influential and important to talk to, frantic boasting about one's responsibilities and influence, attempts to impress with one's power and knowledge – all these are indicators that the speaker has put not only their trust but their whole heart in the things of this world: not material possessions, perhaps, but influence and power, position and authority – just as burdensome and equally without a place in the kingdom of heaven.

## Exercise

How important to you is your standing and authority in your community? What networks of power are you part of and what is your position with them? You might feel that you have a position in the world, or you might feel that you no longer do, or that you never had. You might be surprised when you begin to reflect upon your life and the influence you have on the people you share it with. Experiment by visiting a place or going where you are unknown – go to a church you don't know or attend a group which is new to you. How does it feel to be treated as a newcomer? Do you feel assessed or judged by the people who are there? What do you think they are basing their judgements on? How might this affect your behaviour towards others in the future? What might it feel like to enter Christ's presence? What will he base his assessment on and how will you fare?

# Living generously

**But a man named Ananias, with the consent of his wife Sapphira, sold a piece of property; with his wife's knowledge, he kept back some of the proceeds, and brought only a part and laid it at the apostles' feet. 'Ananias,' Peter asked, 'why has Satan filled your heart to lie to the Holy Spirit and to keep back part of the proceeds of the land? While it remained unsold, did it not remain your own? And after it was sold, were not the proceeds at your disposal? How is it that you have contrived this deed in your heart? You did not lie to us but to God!' Now when Ananias heard these words, he fell down and died. And great fear seized all who heard of it.**
ACTS 5:1–5

Giving is a complicated affair. Research has shown that the wealthier people are, the less likely they are to share their wealth with others. It is believed that having money somehow inhibits the neural pathways which enable empathy for another's situation. Perhaps wealth provides such a feeling of security, an assumption that there are few problems which money cannot solve, that the person feels somehow cushioned from the rest of the world, as if there were an invisible barrier which prevents them from sympathising with or understanding others. Maybe wealth gained by struggle or hard work increases a reluctance to share on the grounds that if it were so hard-won it should not be given away lightly and that others could also achieve wealth through hard work. None of these arguments hold water with Jesus, who firmly tells us to give generously. In fact, giving is assumed – it is how to give that needs explanation: 'When you give alms,' we are told, 'do not let your left hand know what your right hand is doing' (Matthew 6:3). Not if, but when. Jesus' message is based on the precept that just as we have received so much from God, so in our turn should we give freely – of love, respect, tolerance, understanding and the material things that enable life to be sustained.

Within this context, the violence and retribution heaped upon Ananias and Sapphira might seem more understandable. By with-holding some of their property and then compounding the offence by lying about it, this couple have gone against all tradition. By not sharing all they have, they have broken trust with the new community, to the detriment of its physical and spiritual well-being. They have refused to commit themselves wholeheartedly to this new Christ-centred life, resolving to squirrel away some reserves in case of disaster.

The life of contentment involves letting go of all that blocks the path of relationship with Christ. It involves resolving to feel no greed or acquisitiveness, no fear of a materially poor future, but instead an attitude of thanksgiving for all that has been given to us and an acknowledgement of God's grace in his gifts to us, however great or small we may feel them to be. The path to contentment involves helping others to make the same journey by offering them support and understanding, by giving those without anything enough material security that they can focus on more than mere survival. The path to contentment involves giving – generous giving, sacrificial giving – of time, energy, wealth and love.

## Exercise

Take an honest look at the amount of giving you do. Do not be afraid to take into account your gift of time and energy, but make sure you are honest about your financial gift too. Zacchaeus gave half of all he had to the poor; the new community in Jerusalem shared all they had; the widow gave a mite. How much you give is up to you, but it may well be that God wants you to give more than you can easily part with.

# Section VI

# The path of contentment: keeping focused

It is a truism that the more familiar we are with a habit or a way of life, the easier it is to become distracted from it. With practice comes ease, and with ease comes a disregard for the way. This section helps us not to lose focus on our journey to contentment, whatever the distractions and temptations that try to lure us away from the true path. The blandishments of those who do not see the importance of our journey, like Christian's so-called friend Mr Worldly Wiseman, must be resisted. We must face up to our anxieties and fears, not allowing them to divert us from the true path – it is Fear which drives Christian towards the Slough of Despond so precipitately that he misses the steps and falls right into it. Above all, we must focus on God, our true helper and friend, who will lead us along right paths towards his kingdom.

# Not going with the crowd

Early in the morning he came again to the temple. All the people came to him and he sat down and began to teach them. The scribes and the Pharisees brought a woman who had been caught in adultery; and making her stand before all of them, they said to him, 'Teacher, this woman was caught in the very act of committing adultery. Now in the law Moses commanded us to stone such women. Now what do you say?' They said this to test him, so that they might have some charge to bring against him. Jesus bent down and wrote with his finger on the ground. When they kept on questioning him, he straightened up and said to them, 'Let anyone among you who is without sin be the first to throw a stone at her.' And once again he bent down and wrote on the ground. When they heard it, they went away, one by one, beginning with the elders; and Jesus was left alone with the woman standing before him. Jesus straightened up and said to her, 'Woman, where are they? Has no one condemned you?' She said, 'No one, sir.' And Jesus said, 'Neither do I condemn you. Go your way, and from now on do not sin again.'

JOHN 8:2–11

What a mob Jesus faced! Expecting simply to spend some time with disciples new and old, teaching and encouraging them, helping them move forward in their understanding of the kingdom, Jesus is instead called upon to make a judgement upon somebody's life. The

Pharisees, who did not disguise the fact that they were trying to trip Jesus up, demand to know what his action will be against a woman caught in a crime for which the punishment is severe indeed. The woman's guilt is not disputed, nor is Jesus asked to defend her – she is simply a pawn in the hands of those who wish Jesus ill. Surrounded by people waiting for him to make an answer they can seize upon to condemn him in turn, it would not be surprising if Jesus were to bow to pressure and agree that the law of Moses should be enacted.

But, of course, he doesn't. He steps away mentally from the crowd, allowing himself, and them, time to pause and reflect. Emotions have been aroused by the cry of the mob. Rage and hatred – feelings that can suppress our innate humanity and love – are being directed at Jesus and the woman, and possibly also at other events in each person's life. In taking time to pause, Jesus has given these emotions a chance to die down and given common sense and proportion a chance to re-emerge. It is into this pause that Jesus speaks, reminding everyone present that they too are sinners – maybe not in the same way as the woman they are accusing, but sinners nonetheless. And any charity they afford to this woman is only that which they would in turn passionately desire for themselves.

Although we no longer stone people to death, western civilisation still finds ways to hurt and destroy the happiness and even lives of others through the actions of crowds. For some years now there has been a growing anxiety about the effect of social media on our young people. On top of all the normal demands of adolescence – working out an identity separate from parents, changing and growing physically and mentally, the pressures of school work – this generation is facing a challenge which previous generations did not have to experience. It now seems to be part of a young person's life that almost every moment of it should be documented. Photographs of not just parties and outings, but also meals and drinks, clothing choices and everyday activities, are now exhibited to an ever-wider audience. More stressful still, this audience is encouraged to respond to an individual's choices by 'liking' or forwarding, adding comments or criticisms. Small wonder that so many teenagers are lost in a desperate scramble to gain and retain that nebulous concept of popularity. Making decisions for oneself, relying on experience, judgement and the advice of the wise, must be harder than ever.

The journey towards contentment involves resolving to stand apart from the crowd, allowing time for emotions to subside, so that careful, considered reflection and reasoning can take place. It involves listening to the quiet voices of wisdom and experience, of love and tolerance – voices which often get shouted down in the noise of the multitude. But contentment is found not only in not allowing one's own self to become swayed by the desires and opinions of others, but also in supporting those who are unable to cope alone with the pressures of the crowd, standing alongside the lone voice or reassuring those who seek the right way rather than the way of the majority.

## Exercise

If you use social media, pray each time you use it that your words and reactions will be loving and thoughtful. Ask for God's help in remembering that at the other end of every interaction there is a real person, whose life may be affected by your opinion and who is owed respect and dignity.

# 26

# Who touched me?

As he went, the crowds pressed in on him. Now there was a woman who had been suffering from haemorrhages for twelve years; and though she had spent all she had on physicians, no one could cure her. She came up behind him and touched the fringe of his clothes, and immediately her haemorrhage stopped. Then Jesus asked, 'Who touched me?' When all denied it, Peter said, 'Master, the crowds surround you and press in on you.' But Jesus said, 'Someone touched me; for I noticed that power had gone out from me.' When the woman saw that she could not remain hidden, she came trembling; and falling down before him, she declared in the presence of all the people why she had touched him, and how she had been immediately healed. He said to her, 'Daughter, your faith has made you well; go in peace.'

LUKE 8:42–48

Watching my teenage son do his homework causes me both to laugh and to despair. I laugh because of the number of time-wasting distractions he puts into effect before actually settling down to a specific piece of work. He has to clear his desk, find out from his friends what the homework actually is and get them to send over a copy of what he needs because he has left his book at school. He has to find his phone charger and plug it in, taking the opportunity to check his status on social media and send a few pictures of himself flying through the ether. He then decides he is hungry, or might be hungry, and sets off to find a plate of food, hoovering up whatever he can find in the fridge. Finally, a good 20 minutes after the beginning of this exercise, he is ready to work. I despair because of the time wasted, the energy dissipated and the thought that if he had only got on with it, he would be finished by now!

So I admire deeply how Jesus, walking through a dense crowd which presses all about him, can remain oblivious to their calls upon his attention. He has a task to carry out – a child is sick to the point of death and only he can save her. But then, in the midst of the pushing and the confusion, the shouting and press of the people around him, he stops and turns his attention to someone right in the middle of the crowd. Why does he do it? Why does he allow himself to be distracted by her and not by anyone else? Surely other people would have wanted to talk to him – people he ignored so he could reach he girl before it was too late. Even if there were no one else, then the need of this woman is not as great as that of the girl – after all, she has lived with the illness for years. She is chronically, not acutely, sick. Furthermore, on a scale of priorities, she must be well down the list – elderly and poor, even if she were healed she has very few years left to live, and possibly nothing useful to contribute to society. By all logical, secular criteria, she could reasonably be ignored.

But not by Jesus – for his priorities, as has been demonstrated time and again, are not those of the world. He doesn't measure people by how wealthy or influential they are, even by how much they contribute to their community or family. He measures them by who they are, how great their need is and the depth of their faith. So he stops, he turns and the woman is healed.

Like my son, distraction will be part of our faith journey. It is all too easy to be distracted from our main task and to allow the priorities and standards of the secular world to affect our judgement of what is important. It takes so much energy to focus on the main thing. Even Jesus feels the power go out of him when the woman touches the hem of his garment. But maintaining our priorities is an important life task – it will affect the entire direction of our lives: the decisions we make, the obligations we undertake, the people we love and serve. Sometimes these priorities require more energy and focus to maintain than we can easily give – we must guard against distractions and not be seduced on to easier paths.

But at the same time, we must remain alert to the opportunities offered to us to love and serve others, not trampling over their needs in our rush to achieve our own goals, but respecting the faith journey of others and helping them where we can. In fact, turning aside may be part of our journey; stopping to help may become one of our priorities. If this is the case, then we can do as Jesus does, taking as much time as we need, focusing on the situation of the moment, allowing the grace of God to work in and through us, dwelling in the peace and contentment which comes from knowing we are being the people he has designed us to be.

## Exercise

Write out the below verse on a piece of paper and keep it with you in your wallet or purse. Periodically throughout the day, remind yourselves of his words and see how what you are doing measures up to these two great priorities.

He asked him, 'Which commandment is the first of all?' Jesus answered, 'The first is, "Hear, O Israel: the Lord our God, the Lord is one; you shall love the Lord your God with all your heart, and with all your soul, and with all your mind, and with all your strength." The second is this, "You shall love your neighbour as yourself." There is no other commandment greater than these.'
MARK 12:28–31

# Remaining certain of your purpose

**'But strive first for the kingdom of God and his righteousness, and all these things will be given to you as well. So do not worry about tomorrow, for tomorrow will bring worries of its own. Today's trouble is enough for today.'**
MATTHEW 6:33–34

A member of a local church spoke to me recently about her concern for her worshipping community. 'I don't really know the direction it's heading in,' she said. 'It seems to have no idea of where it is going or what its purpose is. It's full of different people with all sorts of views who are all striving for their voices to be heard and for the church to be taken in the particular direction they see as the right one.' I sympathised with her and with her community. In our modern world, with its freedom of lifestyle choices and its seemingly opt-in approach to principles and commitments, it can seem as if the church as a body and its members as individuals are adrift on a sea of conflicting advice, pushed in every direction by the winds of fashion, with no clear idea as to its destination. It is hard to be contented when you are uncertain, when different paths are presented to you almost daily, all offering different levels of personal and community engagement, many promising apparently miraculous levels of reward.

In this famous passage from Matthew, Jesus speaks reassuringly down through the centuries to generations of confused and anxious believers, uncertain as to the way forward. Look first to the kingdom, he tells us in words that will comfort and challenge, for the kingdom of God has great expectations of us as individuals and communities. Look first to carrying out those tasks and working on those relationships which seem to bring the kingdom of God nearer. Look first to the poor, the needy among you; look first to loving your neighbour in whatever way you can, alongside loving yourself and valuing what you can contribute. Above all, look first to God, because if you can fix your eyes on him, the way ahead will become clear.

Contentment comes when we are sure of our goals. With our goals in place, we can see the direction we need to take in order to achieve them. The path may be challenging, but the way will be clear and everything else, we are promised, will fall into place.

## Exercise

Take an empty glass or clear jar, of medium size. Take some larger stones, some small pebbles and some sand or grit. Taking the large stones, identify each one with a priority for your life – this could be care of your family, your church or community work, or an obligation to a neighbour. Once you have done this, set aside a pebble for each of the things that give your life meaning – your hobbies, your less important friendships, care of your home. Finally, apportion some sand or grit to the things that fill up the rest of your life – running errands, watching films, checking your phone.

Begin by placing the sand or grit in the jar first, then the pebbles, then finally the larger stones. You may well find that these large stones will not all fit in the jar – your priorities have been crowded out by the busyness of small tasks. If, however, you begin by placing the large stones in the jar, you will discover that the gaps between can be filled easily with the pebbles and then the sand.

Jesus promises us that if we keep our focus and maintain our priorities, then 'all these things will be given to you as well'.

# Make God your priority

> 'Now therefore revere the Lord, and serve him in sincerity and in faithfulness; put away the gods that your ancestors served beyond the River and in Egypt, and serve the Lord. Now if you are unwilling to serve the Lord, choose this day whom you will serve, whether the gods your ancestors served in the region beyond the River or the gods of the Amorites in whose land you are living; but as for me and my household, we will serve the Lord.'
>
> JOSHUA 24:14–15

Keeping to our priorities can be a very challenging experience. Daily we are enticed away from our true path by the blandishments of the secular world. Why gather with the body of Christ, when the shops of the town centre are open and enticing, luring us in to try to satisfy our hunger with purchases of attractive objects? Why look to help the lonely or the elderly of the community, when the influential and successful are so much more exciting and rewarding, with their promises of borrowed popularity? And why look to an unspecified time in the future when God's kingdom will be revealed on earth, when all around us other goals appear easier and more achievable? The reassurance we need and the certainty we seek are found in many places throughout the Bible, but perhaps nowhere more strongly than here in the words of Joshua to his people, newly arrived in the land of Canaan.

In the previous few verses, Joshua has told the people their story up to the present moment. He has reminded them of the story of

Abraham and the land of Canaan, of the birth of Jacob and Esau. He has spoken of Moses and the liberation of the children of Israel and the journey through the wilderness to the point of crossing the Jordan. Their recent battle triumphs are still fresh in the people's minds – the defeat of the Amorites, the Perizzites, the Canaanites, the Hittites, the Girgashites, the Hivites and the Jebusites (v. 11). They are reminded that it is through God's will that they have entered this land: 'I gave you a land on which you had not laboured, and towns that you had not built, and you live in them; you eat the fruit of vineyards and olive groves that you did not plant' (v. 13).

But all this was not accomplished by the children of Israel alone – indeed, it was often achieved despite them! For God was behind it all, honouring his covenant to his people, leading them to the land he had promised them generations ago. And it is in the honouring of this promise that Joshua exhorts his people to place their trust. Mindful of all that has been done for them, they must respond in worship and service: 'As for me and my household we will serve the Lord.'

In the same way, we can look back on all that God has done for us, the covenant of love and forgiveness created through Christ's sacrifice, and place our trust in the coming of his kingdom, working to bring it to fruition.

## Exercise

If you can, look up the hymns 'Rivers' (Brenton Prigge, 2005) and 'Choose this day the one you'll follow' (Carolyn Winfrey Gillette, 2015). Both of these are based on Joshua's statement and use traditional melodies. Try writing a hymn or song yourself, using a favourite tune and adding words which express the resolution of Joshua, owning it for yourself.

**29**

# Put aside anxieties and pains

> Now, discipline always seems painful rather than pleasant at the time, but later it yields the peaceful fruit of righteousness to those who have been trained by it. Therefore lift your drooping hands and strengthen your weak knees, and make straight paths for your feet, so that what is lame may not be put out of joint, but rather be healed.
>
> HEBREWS 12:11–13

One of the joys of being a parish priest in the Church of England is the duty laid upon us to say morning and evening prayer. It isn't always possible to say these in public, but often it is. To gather with a small group of Christians first thing in the morning and pray together is a privilege indeed. The rhythm of the liturgical seasons, the daily Bible readings and seasonal prayers and canticles give an order and structure for the day, and they remind us of who we are and whom we serve. Such small gatherings allow for personal support and discussion and a greater knowledge of one's prayer companions. The insights and comments of the fellow pilgrims have been a great support over the years, and I have many treasured memories.

One such memory is brought to mind whenever I read this passage from Hebrews. Verses 12–13 draw upon Isaiah 35, which is used as a canticle, called 'A Song of the Wilderness', in the morning prayer, recited daily throughout the season of Advent. I remember well one stalwart of morning prayer, who met me in an icy cold church every morning, greeting me always with a cheerful grin and encouraging words. She was quite elderly and rather infirm. Her recent knee operation had been difficult and the results painful, but she struggled gallantly with her daily exercises, inwardly wincing occasionally as she bent her knees to sit down. At the end of one particularly cold gathering, she said, 'I often recite the Song of the Wilderness to myself, asking God to "make firm my feeble knees". I find it helps, somehow.' Her dearest wish was to be able to kneel to take Communion, which she did, joyfully, on Christmas Day.

Journeying on the road to contentment will not be easy. There will be times when our spiritual disciplines seem dreary and harsh, when we feel no joy in our undertakings, no reward for the sacrifices we are making daily – whether these are to lead a simpler way of life, to offer services to those in need or to maintain a routine of prayer, reflection and study. Aches and pains can be spiritual and emotional as well as physical, and it is easy to allow these to weaken or even overwhelm our personal disciplines, but we are reminded that the rewards are great – the peaceful fruit of righteousness and the healing of that which is lame within us.

## Exercise

You are now over halfway on your journey. How has this been so far? Look back over your journal – what has changed for you in this time? Have any of your prayer requests been answered and in what way? Look again at your prayer space – does it need refreshing or changing? Do the books and objects which you found helpful at the beginning of your journey still offer support? Perhaps you could plan an outing to a bookshop or library to spend time browsing new Christian books, studies or texts – whatever you find useful.

# Section VII

## The path of contentment: facing afflictions

John Bunyan wrote *The Pilgrim's Progress* while he was in jail, imprisoned for over twelve years for his religious nonconformity. It became his most famous work, has been translated into over 200 languages and has never been out of print. What a feat of determination and courage this must have been, to write cheerfully and consistently in a place so bleak and forlorn of hope! He also wrote his autobiography during this time.

No one's life is completely free from trials and misfortunes – what matters is less what happens to us and more how we react to adverse circumstances. In this section we explore attitudes towards affliction, drawing courage from the example of those who have gone before us and looking to the future with hope. We look for ways of maintaining our faith in times of difficulty, holding on to our belief in a compassionate and forgiving God, who will lead us through dark times into his marvellous light.

**30**

# Three times I was shipwrecked

Five times I have received from the Jews the forty lashes minus one. Three times I was beaten with rods. Once I received a stoning. Three times I was shipwrecked; for a night and a day I was adrift at sea; on frequent journeys, in danger from rivers, danger from bandits, danger from my own people, danger from Gentiles, danger in the city, danger in the wilderness, danger at sea, danger from false brothers and sisters; in toil and hardship, through many a sleepless night, hungry and thirsty, often without food, cold and naked. And, besides other things, I am under daily pressure because of my anxiety for all the churches.

2 CORINTHIANS 11:24–28

What a litany of suffering and hardship, undergone in order to spread the story of the life, death and resurrection of Christ and the hope that this must bring to all people! And yet Paul does not appear to be telling the Corinthians about his tribulations in order to gain sympathy or to excuse himself for work not accomplished, journeys not made. There is a complete lack of such self-consciousness in his cheerful recitation of all the horrors that he has endured in the name of Christ. Paul simply wants to make a point. And what are we supposed to take from this, apart from a feeling of humble thankfulness that we will in all probability not be asked to undergo suffering on a similar scale?

The minor indignations and humiliations that we might suffer because of our faith – the occasional sneering remarks about our church-going habits or pointed criticism about the failings of the church, with the implication that this is somehow our fault – these fade into insignificance besides the beatings and stonings, the imprisonments and shipwrecks experienced by Paul. That all this can happen to such a prayer warrior as Paul, one who went from 'ravaging the church' (Acts 8:3) to being chosen by God to bring his name 'before Gentiles and kings and before the people of Israel' (Acts 9:15), should both comfort and appal us. We are comforted in the knowledge that any afflictions which we bear are not imposed as punishment for sin or failure, and appalled at the amount of suffering those who seek to share the good news must endure. It seems almost as if suffering is a requirement for Christians – it was for Paul: at his conversion, God said, 'I myself will show him how much he must suffer for the sake of my name' (Acts 9:16).

Paul's attitude to this suffering may also serve as an example to us – difficult though it will be to achieve. Paul's cheerful acceptance does not diminish his pain, but his refusal to dwell upon it prevents it from taking over the whole of his life. He has experienced traumatic and hideous things – he will do so again in the future – but he bears this knowledge with fortitude and does not allow it to damage his relationship with those he serves. The poison of resentment is not allowed to corrupt his attitude of loving service – he rejoices at the good fortune of others while bearing stoically his own circumstances.

We know what Paul could not – that his actions would lead to his death – but we also know that the achievements of his lifetime lived on long after this death, inspiring, teaching and encouraging all those who walk the Christian way.

## Exercise

I cannot be so presumptuous as to offer a way of approaching suffering to those who are experiencing mental, physical or emotional pain. All I can write, drawing from my own experience, is that much of the fear associated with pain is due to our anxious anticipation of future, worsening pain. The courage required to face pain is drained by imaginings and foreboding. A mind fixed on experiencing the moment, both the good and the bad that it contains, will have more strength to endure than that which ranges freely, building 'worst-case scenarios' with increasing despair. 'We are God's children now' (1 John 3:2), and it is in the now that we must dwell, looking for the hope and the peace that awareness of Christ's presence alongside us, sharing in our suffering and working to redeem it, will bring.

# Looking for the silver lining

Gracious is the Lord, and righteous; our God is merciful. The Lord protects the simple; when I was brought low, he saved me. Return, O my soul, to your rest, for the Lord has dealt bountifully with you. For you have delivered my soul from death, my eyes from tears, my feet from stumbling. I walk before the Lord in the land of the living. I kept my faith, even when I said, 'I am greatly afflicted.'

PSALM 116:5–10

What a beautiful passage this is, full of heartfelt thanksgiving for a life delivered from death. We do not know what it was that brought the psalmist low: it might have been an illness, suffered by the writer or a loved one; particular life circumstances might have conspired to reduce the writer to potential destitution; or perhaps life in its totality, with all its complications and demands, had become overwhelming to the point of despair. We do know, however, that this desperate situation is over and that the writer now walks 'in the land of the living'. We are also assured, with pride, that even during the darkest times the writer kept his faith. I wonder whether, looking back on his experience, he can see whether any good has come from it. I have always found it a particular challenge to be told that suffering can be beneficial, with the implication that such pain or grief as I was experiencing was due to God either testing me or teaching me, rebuking me or training me. Surely a loving God, who wants only the best for each one of us, does not inflict suffering in such a pragmatic way? Surely a loving God would find a different way to teach us the lessons we need to learn?

We do not know the full answer to the mystery of suffering, for this will not be revealed to us until our life here on this earth has ended and we have passed into another realm, one where we will see God face-to-face and not 'through a glass, darkly' (1 Corinthians 13:12, KJV). There, we are promised, all suffering and sorrow will be swept away and all will be made right. Until then, however, we must live with the mystery and try to keep our faith, even in the darkest of times. For it can be during these dark times that the light of God's love for us is seen most clearly, whether in the comfort of friends or family, the routine of daily life, the support of a church community or the remembrance of Christ's death and suffering for our sakes. And when the hard times have passed, for they surely will, and the pain, if it has not died away completely, has eased somewhat, then perhaps we can look back on our time of suffering and see whether there are lessons that can be learnt from it.

In my experience as a minister, I have seen that those who experience loss or great pain are inevitably changed by that experience. In some cases, their personalities become twisted or damaged. They might become suspicious of good times, dubious about loving actions. Their suffering might lead to an inability to love further or to commit to other people or communities. Or it might take them towards frantic campaigning or driven fundraising, frenetic socialising or abuse of alcohol and drug dependency. For these people, gentle acceptance and deep and constant loving tolerance and forbearance are required, while prayers for their healing continue.

Others, however, find that their suffering takes them in a different direction. They might change jobs or occupations, seeking to put right situations and circumstances which might lead others into suffering. Their priorities in life might change, focusing perhaps on people and communities rather than possessions and wealth. Their suffering might give them an extra dimension of understanding and empathy, a softening of the hard shell which so many of us develop in order to cope with the battle of daily life. These people, although they would never have wished their suffering to happen, manage to draw out of it some benefit for themselves and for others, some goodness. The suffering thus becomes transformed, as it transforms those who endured it, and new hope for the future is born.

## Exercise

This exercise might be too challenging for some people – if you find yourself becoming upset or disturbed, do not continue.

Take an incident in your life which has caused you to suffer. You may not want to choose an extreme example, such as a death or severe illness, but focus instead on an unpleasant or mildly upsetting incident. It might be an occasion when you were hurt by a comment or when a project you undertook did not go as well as expected, or it might just be an embarrassing social situation.

Reflect on the situation, bringing it back from your memory. What made it difficult or upsetting? How did you react? How did others react? Looking back on the incident, how might you have reacted differently – would this have changed the outcome? What have you learnt from your experience? How might you react in the future?

Try to describe what you have learnt in one sentence or one word. If you prefer, draw or make a collage of your learning.

# Complain to God if you need to

**But I, O Lord, cry out to you; in the morning my prayer comes before you. O Lord, why do you cast me off? Why do you hide your face from me? Wretched and close to death from my youth up, I suffer your terrors; I am desperate. Your wrath has swept over me; your dread assaults destroy me. They surround me like a flood all day long; from all sides they close in on me. You have caused friend and neighbour to shun me; my companions are in darkness.**

PSALM 88:13–18

It is difficult, not to say impossible, to remain perfectly contented at all times with one's situation and circumstances. Indeed, it is not even advisable, since absolute contentment can easily slide into apathy, and your spiritual journey could drift slowly to a halt as you cease to find the impetus required to continue your progress. On the other hand, however, extreme suffering, anxieties and the anguish of crises or accidents can have the same effect, causing us to come to a standstill while we survey what appears to be the destruction of the landscape of our lives. We studied previously the benefits – the absolute imperative, in fact – of continuing to hold fast to our faith in times of difficulty and struggle, not ceasing to trust in the working for good of our creator and Father.

The writer of Psalm 116 declares proudly that not once did his faith waiver despite his misfortunes, and we should take up that challenge of continuing to declare our faith in a good and loving God, despite apparent evidence to the contrary. However, a steadfast faith does not mean a constant cheerfulness. The writer of Psalm 116 and the writer of today's psalm both feel free to complain vigorously to God at the way their fortunes have turned out. In fact, Psalm 88 declares at some length the grievous nature of the writer's circumstances: 'I suffer your terrors; I am desperate.' He does not withhold from placing the blame for his situation firmly at the feet of God: 'You have caused friend and neighbour to shun me.' He does not understand God's behaviour and is upset and angry at its apparent injustice: 'O Lord, why do you cast me off? Why do you hide your face from me?'

This example of an angry outcry at apparently causeless misfortune is not the only one in the Psalms – indeed, this book of the Bible is full of them. Anger, bitterness, envy and disappointment all find an outlet in the poetry of the psalms as the writers rail against a God who appears to allow suffering, misfortune, injustice and defeat. Yet among all this outcry remains a steadfast faith in a God whose back is broad enough to take all sorts of abuse from his children, whom he loves. The anger expressed is always against a background of a steadfast faith, a refusal to give up, a determination to keep to the covenant, despite not understanding how God is keeping to his side of the agreement.

The writers of the psalms, in expressing their anger and disappoint-ment, give us permission to do so as well – better an outpouring of emotion than the empty flatness of disbelief; better a vivid and energetic engagement with God than a cold distancing. For after the outpouring of emotion comes the return of quiet trust. The angry turning away becomes a seeking of the comfort that only God can give, as we return to the one who loves us truly and perfectly, for all that we are.

> For God alone my soul waits in silence; from him comes my salvation. He alone is my rock and my salvation, my fortress; I shall never be shaken.
>
> PSALM 62:1–2

## Exercise

Next time you are feeling angry or annoyed at the way things have turned out – either for you personally, for something in the lives of your friends and neighbours or for a world issue – try shouting a psalm! Find a place, far away from others, where you can express yourself as loudly as you wish, then allow yourself to shout out your feelings to God. You can use your own words or those of the psalmist – try 88 or 116 for starters, but there are plenty of others. When you have finished, however, repeat softly to yourself the words of Psalm 62:1–2, reminding yourself that God's love is constant and never-ending, and that you may rest with confidence in his love: 'How precious is your steadfast love, O God! All people may take refuge in the shadow of your wings' (Psalm 36:7).

# Seek help

Then Amalek came and fought with Israel at Rephidim. Moses said to Joshua, 'Choose some men for us and go out; fight with Amalek. Tomorrow I will stand on the top of the hill with the staff of God in my hand.' So Joshua did as Moses told him, and fought with Amalek, while Moses, Aaron, and Hur went up to the top of the hill. Whenever Moses held up his hand, Israel prevailed; and whenever he lowered his hand, Amalek prevailed. But Moses' hands grew weary; so they took a stone and put it under him, and he sat on it. Aaron and Hur held up his hands, one on one side, and the other on the other side; so his hands were steady until the sun set. And Joshua defeated Amalek and his people with the sword.

EXODUS 17:8–13

One of the major problems facing many churches today is the overwhelming workload of their ministers. Faced with rising costs, the burden of fundraising, administrative issues as well as the regular round of services and pastoral care, mission initiatives and discipleship programmes, there is always something more that a church leader can do, and their task is never at an end. Members of church communities might also find themselves in similar situations – a faithful children's leader might find themselves longing for a Sunday when they might be part of the main church worship; the person who leads the coffee rota might feel they never want to pour another cup of coffee again. There might be circumstances which arise in people's personal or work lives which mean that the time they can give to other matters is suddenly limited, but their contribution to a programme or event is so vital that they feel they cannot cease to offer their time and energy for fear of collapse. In some cases, collapse is exactly what does happen – a person might reach the end of their endurance, the limits of their energy, and discover they have arrived at burnout.

The assumption of too many tasks and obligations, however beneficial they are to the community or group, is not part of the journey to contentment. A realistic recognition of one's limitations and a willingness to ask for help when it is needed are both integral and essential, if a traveller on the road to contentment is not to subside in a heap by the side of the path, worn out by burdens and wearied by too many duties. Sometimes a task will be beyond our skill or outside our area of knowledge and expertise; sometimes it will be something we are capable of doing but we lack the energy or time to undertake it alone. In these cases, struggling along by oneself is not the answer, and it is time to reach out for help and support.

This can be very challenging, especially for someone who has always prided themselves on their independence or their ability to get things done. It can be a humbling matter to admit the need for help – our pride may feel wounded, our self-esteem damaged. Just as it clearly took Moses some time to acknowledge that he could not be solely responsible for the course of the battle against the Amalekites, so it can take us some time to acknowledge our shortcomings, our weariness or our lack of time. But a call for help should not be an occasion for shame; it should be a recognition of the contribution of others. By holding up the hands of Moses, Aaron and Hur ensured the success of the battle; thus victory became a group effort rather than a solo task.

# Exercise

At the beginning of our journey, we looked at simplifying our lives and establishing those things which were priorities for us. Look again at the tasks and obligations you have decided upon. Is it all working well? Do you find you have enough time to undertake everything? Do you feel overwhelmed by all that you have to do? Are there areas in which you could ask for help? Consider prayerfully how you might go about seeking help and from whom you might obtain it.

Be grateful also for those people who do help and support you – whether by the things they do, the services they provide or their prayers and loving actions.

Make a set of concertina people. Fold a rectangular piece of paper – A5 is a good size – about five times concertina-style. Draw a figure on the first fold of the paper, making sure the hands and feet (or arms and legs if it is a simple figure) touch the outside edges. Cut round the figure, being careful not to cut where the arms and legs touch the sides. When you open out the paper you will have five people holding hands. On these figures write the names of all those who help you. Or you might want to give each figure a different task, writing the names of all those who help you in your prayer life on one figure, for example, or simply give a name to each figure. Place the concertina people in your prayer space and remember to give thanks for them.

# Take up your cross

Then he said to them all, 'If any want to become my followers, let them deny themselves and take up their cross daily and follow me. For those who want to save their life will lose it, and those who lose their life for my sake will save it. What does it profit them if they gain the whole world, but lose or forfeit themselves? Those who are ashamed of me and of my words, of them the Son of Man will be ashamed when he comes in his glory and the glory of the Father and of the holy angels. But truly I tell you, there are some standing here who will not taste death before they see the kingdom of God.'

LUKE 9:23–27

There is today in the secular world a huge expectation of happiness. We assume we will be happy and contented most of the time. We assume we will not suffer unduly from any physical or mental illness. We assume we will not experience any serious degree of want. After a while, the assumption turns into presumption – our physical and mental well-being becomes not a gift but a right, not a privilege but something that is owed to us. If for some reason any measure of happiness is denied us, we are outraged and affronted and look around for someone who can take the blame for this unnatural situation. I suspect this is not a new thing – in fact, it is almost a survival instinct, because if we did not believe that fundamentally things were all going to be alright, we might not even want to fight to stay alive or find any reason to have children to continue the line.

What a shock it must have been for the followers of Christ, therefore, to be told that their expectation should be not good fortune but tribulation, not an easy life but a difficult one, probably ending in death. What an act of courage for those first disciples to say, 'Yes. That's okay. We need to be pushed outside our comfort zone. We need to let go of the things that keep us safe – our property, our relationships, our lives which are diminished but comfortable. We need to leave all that behind and step out on a new journey, embracing whatever lies before us, aware that it will be difficult and dangerous but doing it nonetheless.' The way of the cross is not an easy one, but it is the path which leads to eternal life. The way of the cross will involve accepting affliction without seeking to lay the blame on someone else – not even God. It involves giving up certainty, even the 'certainty' that illness and misfortune are a punishment inflicted on those who have done wrong. It involves seeking God in whatever circumstances befall us, knowing that he will be there in the midst of the suffering, whether we see him or not.

The great theologian Dietrich Bonhoeffer's life was ended for him in a German prison. An authority on suffering, his viewpoint transforms this passage:

> To endure the cross is not a tragedy. It is not an accident; it is a necessity. It is the suffering which is an essential part of the specifically Christian life. The cross is laid on every Christian. Firstly we must abandon the attachments to this world, then we surrender ourselves to God's will. The cross is not a terrible end to an otherwise God-fearing and happy life, but it meets us at the beginning of our communion with Christ, for it is Christ whom the disciple finds as he picks up his cross.

## Exercise

The cross is a symbol for Christians of both suffering and forgiveness, sin and absolution, death and resurrection. What symbols remind you of your suffering, and how might you transform them? Take an object, a prayer, a picture or a piece of music that reminds you of a time in your life when you have experienced difficulties. As you look or listen, offer up your experience to God, asking him to transform it. Draw or trace with your finger the sign of the cross over your object or picture, or make the shape of it in the air. Ask God for acceptance of the struggle that is part of life, for the grace to surrender to his will for you and the strength to follow his way.

# Keep your faith

Immediately he made the disciples get into the boat and go on ahead to the other side, while he dismissed the crowds. And after he had dismissed the crowds, he went up the mountain by himself to pray. When evening came, he was there alone, but by this time the boat, battered by the waves, was far from the land, for the wind was against them. And early in the morning he came walking towards them on the lake. But when the disciples saw him walking on the lake, they were terrified, saying, 'It is a ghost!' And they cried out in fear. But immediately Jesus spoke to them and said, 'Take heart, it is I; do not be afraid.'

Peter answered him, 'Lord, if it is you, command me to come to you on the water.' He said, 'Come.' So Peter got out of the boat, started walking on the water, and came towards Jesus. But when he noticed the strong wind, he became frightened, and beginning to sink, he cried out, 'Lord, save me!' Jesus immediately reached out his hand and caught him, saying to him, 'You of little faith, why did you doubt?' When they got into the boat, the wind ceased. And those in the boat worshiped him, saying, 'Truly you are the Son of God.'

MATTHEW 14:22–33

It is difficult not to feel sorry for Peter – he tries so hard, but so often gets it wrong. But his mistakes come from his eagerness to understand, his courage to try new things, his willingness to speak out, to say the things that perhaps others are afraid to articulate for fear they might look foolish. And Peter does often look foolish, and sometimes cowardly, but he is nonetheless always there, always by Jesus' side, trying to learn, trying to get a grip on this new way of living which his master is demonstrating to them all. He has his failures – that dreadful time of Jesus' arrest and Peter's betrayal has yet to come, but it looms like a shadow over our reading of all his actions. Knowing as we do that when Peter is put under pressure he will fold, we can catch glimpses of this flaw in his behaviour during the time leading up to Christ's death. Perhaps this occasion is one of those times. We get a glimpse of Peter's intelligence, his quick understanding, his enthusiasm and his willingness to undertake all that Jesus asks of him – but all this is the playing of a paper tiger, its flimsy nature easily revealed. It seems doubly hard that Peter's collapse, his sinking down into the waves of doubt, comes when he is trying so hard to follow Jesus, trying to obey his command, reaching out in faith. But all this effort comes to nothing, and it seems as if he will be swallowed up, to perish in the sea of 'maybe' and 'perhaps not'.

So too can we strive earnestly to step out in faith, doubting our ability to carry on, perhaps, but determined that if we fail, it won't be because we didn't put all our effort and energy into the project. In such circumstances, failure, doubt and disappointment hit so much harder, when it seems as if all our hard work has been in vain, Jesus is nowhere to be seen and we will drown beneath the waves.

But Peter doesn't sink, because he knows whose name to call. Even though the strong wind is blowing and his fear is great, he still trusts that Jesus will save him. He realises that he cannot accomplish his task on his own, because his own strength is not enough. He must lean on Jesus, take his hand, allow him to hold his sinking head above the waves until he is safe in the boat once more. And again we learn from this – that we cannot do anything under our own strength, but we must put aside our pride and our independence and lean on the one who will snatch us up from whatever is threatening to overwhelm us and carry us to a place of safety.

## Exercise

Spend some time picturing this episode in your mind. Put yourself in the place of Peter, imagining yourself on a small boat in the middle of the lake. Go through the action step by step. How would you feel as you stepped over the side of the boat? How glorious would it have been to walk on water, treading out over the waves to meet Jesus as he comes towards you? And what fear do you feel as the wind becomes stronger and those waves threaten to overwhelm you and your lungs begin to fill with water and your head sinks beneath the ever-increasing waves? And then Jesus reaches you, and stretches out his hand, and death recedes and your fears fade and you are safe in his hands.

# It will pass

**So we do not lose heart. Even though our outer nature is wasting away, our inner nature is being renewed day by day. For this slight momentary affliction is preparing us for an eternal weight of glory beyond all measure, because we look not at what can be seen but at what cannot be seen; for what can be seen is temporary, but what cannot be seen is eternal.**
2 CORINTHIANS 4:16–18

To keep on 'keeping on' during times of difficulty and suffering is perhaps the hardest thing of all. The immediacy of a doctor's diagnosis or the urgency of an accident or a domestic or relationship crisis all have a momentum about them that helps us to move through those first days. Everything is new and strange; suddenly all the things we accepted as certainties – health, financial security, relationships – are thrown up in the air, like so many playing cards at the end of a trick. We are anxious, afraid even, trying to navigate through unknown waters. But there is often a sort of energy that keeps us going – the shock of the unfamiliar and the need to learn a new vocabulary, whether medical terms, financial jargon or simply being 'I' and not 'we'. The first few days and weeks can pass very quickly, but then it all seems to grind to a halt. The realisation creeps up on us gradually that we are in this for the long haul, that life has changed and may never return to how it was. New and different ways of living have to be learnt; that process is not easy.

It is then that we must lean on our faith, looking to God to give us the strength and courage to continue on this new and difficult pathway.

But we might fear that our faith is not strong enough, that it will not function as a prop, as it is flimsy and frail, unable to support us when we most need it. Perhaps, then, all we can do is look, with Paul, at what cannot be seen, counting on an 'eternal weight of glory beyond all measure'. The light of this glory might seem very faint at the moment, shining as a mere glow on the horizon, but it is there, clouded though the vista might seem.

These loving, reassuring words of Paul remind us that each day brings new hope and that the trials of our afflictions can help to mould us into more perfect human beings. Though the pain of our afflictions might seem to be twisting us out of shape, God sees the inner form and not the outer. Our task is to keep our eyes fixed on the future, which is filled with the promise of his glory.

## Exercise

Plant some seeds or a bulb in a small pot and keep it in your prayer space. As you look at the pot each day, notice that for many days nothing changes. All that is evident is a small pile of dirt in a pot – very uninspiring and not at all a comfort. Gradually, however, you will see evidence of growth – small seedlings sprouting up or the tip of a green shoot just becoming visible above the surface. When the plant is fully grown, its roots in the soil and its bloom pointing at the sky, the time spent in darkness will be justified, as the result is so glorious.

Pray that God will give you the courage and support you need for the dark times and that you will keep your hope fixed on the time to come:

'By the tender mercy of our God, the dawn from on high will break upon us, to give light to those who sit in darkness and in the shadow of death, to guide our feet into the way of peace.'
LUKE 1:78–79

# For everything there is a season

For everything there is a season, and a time for every matter under heaven: a time to be born, and a time to die; a time to plant, and a time to pluck up what is planted; a time to kill, and a time to heal; a time to break down, and a time to build up; a time to weep, and a time to laugh; a time to mourn, and a time to dance; a time to throw away stones, and a time to gather stones together; a time to embrace, and a time to refrain from embracing; a time to seek, and a time to lose; a time to keep, and a time to throw away; a time to tear, and a time to sew; a time to keep silence, and a time to speak; a time to love, and a time to hate; a time for war, and a time for peace.

ECCLESIASTES 3:1–8

My eldest daughter has two children under three. Life for her is hectic, busy and full of surprises – every day a new challenge, every day a new milestone. Conversations with her are full of wonder – why do small children prefer to eat upside down? Why is a puddle irresistible, especially if you are only wearing sandals? Why is sleep something to be avoided at all costs, particularly at bedtimes? Sometimes she is less upbeat, when the sheer hard work of caring for a baby and a toddler have worn her out or she feels as if she will never have any time to herself. When she shares with me some of the triumphs of childcare, I respond with the wisdom of a mother of four – 'Make the most of it; it's just a phase.' To the drudgery of potty-training or dealing with temper tantrums my answer is the same: 'It's just a phase.'

Thirty years of experience have given me a perspective that can be lacking when one is right in the middle of action-packed childrearing – a perspective which is shared by the writer of Ecclesiastes and applied to all phases of life. There will be times in our lives when we are filled with joy, floating on a cloud of success or triumph, love or achievement. There will be times when our lives seem grey with pain or bleak with despair, when the days ahead seem to contain nothing of hope but only a grim endurance and a determination to get through as best one can. To each of these the author writes – it will pass. The good times and the bad, the laughter and the tears.

A contented Christian sits comfortably with both, rejoicing in the good times while remaining aware that they are fleeting and must be seized with both hands and relished, and bearing the bad times, knowing that these too will pass, hopefully leaving in their wake some added wisdom or experience which can be used to improve the lives of others. Contentment is not detachment – each life experience must be entered into wholeheartedly, each moment lived as if it were the last – but it does bring with it an awareness of the long game and a vision of the final destination towards which we all move.

## Exercise

Either search on the internet for landscapes in different seasons or find a book or magazine which contains pictures of these. Try to gather as many different landscapes in all sorts of conditions as you can. Bring them together and place them alongside each other – grouped according to season. Look carefully at these images – which ones do you prefer? Which season is your favourite? See how each one brings different beauties – the ice and cold of winter gradually softening into the pale green of spring, which in turn gives way to the bloom of summer and the maturity of autumn.

Reflect on your own life – which stage do you feel you are at? What are the advantages of each life 'season' and what are its trials? What wisdom have you gained from each life stage – childhood, youth, early and middle adulthood? What would you wish to pass on to others who might be facing the same situations or experiencing the same life events?

# Remember the example of others

When they heard these things, they became enraged and ground their teeth at Stephen. But filled with the Holy Spirit, he gazed into heaven and saw the glory of God and Jesus standing at the right hand of God. 'Look,' he said, 'I see the heavens opened and the Son of Man standing at the right hand of God!' But they covered their ears, and with a loud shout all rushed together against him. Then they dragged him out of the city and began to stone him; and the witnesses laid their coats at the feet of a young man named Saul. While they were stoning Stephen, he prayed, 'Lord Jesus, receive my spirit.' Then he knelt down and cried out in a loud voice, 'Lord, do not hold this sin against them.' When he had said this, he died.

ACTS 7:54–60

I use the Church of England lectionary of readings as part of my daily prayer. It helps me to feel connected to the wider church and also keeps me in the discipline of daily Bible reading. Occasionally I learn surprising things – different saints and martyrs are celebrated on different days, and it is always interesting to research the reason why such a person or group is commemorated and to reflect on their way of life and death. One such example is 2 September – on that day, the Church of England commemorates the martyrs of Papua New Guinea. When the Japanese invaded Papua New Guinea in 1942, the Anglican bishop of New Guinea instructed missionaries to remain at their posts. He wrote to the clergy, 'We must endeavour to carry on our work. God expects this of us. The church at home, which sent us out, will surely expect it of us. The universal church expects it of us. The people whom we serve expect it of us. We could never hold up our faces again if, for our own safety, we all forsook him and fled, when the shadows of the Passion began to gather around him in his spiritual and mystical body, the Church in Papua.' Eight of them were executed, as an example.

We will probably not be asked to die for our faith, but we may well be asked to suffer for it – perhaps not in large ways or magnificent gestures, but in the daily pinpricks of hostile comments from neighbours, or in being asked to give beyond what is comfortable in terms of money, support and service. We will almost certainly experience suffering in other aspects of our lives – no human being gets through life having escaped all suffering. Whether suffering helps us or destroys us, whether it provides an example to others of courage, endurance and faith under fire, or whether it causes others to reflect that if being a Christian brings so much distress, it is better to avoid the faith altogether, is up to each one of us.

The example of Stephen, gazing into the heavens and seeing the glory of God, this vision bringing him the strength to endure everything for the love of God, is as inspirational as the message of the missionaries of Papua New Guinea, who served their church to the end of their lives. We may not be given such a vision or feel we have the courage that is the stuff of martyrs, but we can reflect on such examples and take courage and strength from being part of the same tradition from which they sprang.

# Exercise

Make a collage of your personal heroes. They might be people you know – neighbours, friends or family – or those whose stories you have heard. They might be biblical characters, such as Ruth or David, Paul or Stephen, or they might be fictional ones from favourite novels. As you write their names or glue their portraits on to a large piece of paper, reflect on your reasons for admiring them. What are the qualities which make them heroic to you? Pray for the grace to imitate them in your own life or to find courage from their examples to face your own trials and suffering.

**39**

# Accept God's will

The Lord struck the child that Uriah's wife bore to David, and it became very ill. David therefore pleaded with God for the child; David fasted, and went in and lay all night on the ground. The elders of his house stood beside him, urging him to rise from the ground; but he would not, nor did he eat food with them. On the seventh day the child died. And the servants of David were afraid to tell him that the child was dead; for they said, 'While the child was still alive, we spoke to him, and he did not listen to us; how then can we tell him the child is dead? He may do himself some harm.' But when David saw that his servants were whispering together, he perceived that the child was dead; and David said to his servants, 'Is the child dead?' They said, 'He is dead.'

Then David rose from the ground, washed, anointed himself, and changed his clothes. He went into the house of the Lord, and worshiped; he then went to his own house; and when he asked, they set food before him and he ate. Then his servants said to him, 'What is this thing that you have done? You fasted and wept for the child while it was alive; but when the child died, you rose and ate food.' He said, 'While the child was still alive, I fasted and wept; for I said, "Who knows? The Lord may be gracious to me, and the child may live." But now he is dead; why should I fast? Can I bring him back again? I shall go to him, but he will not return to me.'

2 SAMUEL 12:15–23

My parents were the traditional type of Christian who believed that children should not attend funerals, so I did not experience my first one until I was an adult, with a child of my own. This occasion was made even more poignant by the fact that we were gathered to mourn the death of a little girl named Emma, who had been killed when a car drove into the side of the car she was travelling in. The devastated parents and family were gathered at the front of the church, and a small group of parents who had attended the same toddler group huddled in a back pew, shocked and stunned, not quite believing that the dynamic, lively, chattering toddler, so similar to their own much-loved offspring, would be seen no more.

The vicar, a sympathetic, caring man, began his sermon by telling us that we did not have to worry about the child, because she was with Christ, and in that simple way, so full of faith and love, he swept away our concerns and fears for Emma, so that we could focus on the people who were left behind, whose bitter tears would be shed for many years.

David's faith is strong and vibrant – he believes that his prayers and entreaties will affect the course of things, and that if he fasts and weeps he may yet convince God to spare his son. But the vital, living quality of his faith, which is so much a part of who he is and how he lives his life, is demonstrated not in the way he pleads with God for the life of his son, but in the way that he accepts God's decision so wholeheartedly, absorbing it into his life and setting himself on the right path once more, with scarcely a backwards glance at what might have been.

The death of a child strikes deep into the heart not only of a parent but the family and the whole community, spreading distress and disbelief like ripples from a stone thrown into a still, calm pond, where nothing should have been allowed to disrupt the smoothness of the water. Other deaths, illnesses and misfortunes can strike at all of us, toppling our lives, giving us a stark glimpse of their essential fragility. How hard it is to be like David, to keep praying, to pick up the pieces of our lives and carry on. How difficult, and yet how essential, it is to take up once more the precious gift of hope, the promise of a meeting in eternity to which David holds – although the child cannot be returned to his father, yet 'I shall go to him'.

## Exercise

The agonised prayer of Jesus in the garden of Gethsemane, on the night before he died, strikes a chord in all our hearts: 'My Father, if it is possible, let this cup pass from me.' Yet we too must trust in God's good purposes for us, believing that through Christ, who faced down death for our sake, we will be redeemed and all will be made new, and praying with Jesus: 'Not what I want but what you want' (Matthew 26:39).

> If there is anywhere on earth a lover of God who is always kept safe, I know nothing of it, for it was not shown to me. But this was shown: that in falling and rising again we are always kept in that same precious love.
> Julian of Norwich

# Suffering

Grain is crushed for bread, but one does not thresh it forever; one drives the cartwheel and horses over it, but does not pulverise it. This also comes from the Lord of hosts; he is wonderful in counsel, and excellent in wisdom.

ISAIAH 28:28–29

The mystery of suffering is one of the first issues that new Christians have to grapple with when they begin the journey of faith. In fact, it is one of the issues that all Christians engage with constantly, wherever they are along the way. We debate the reasons why God created a fragile, constantly changing world, one with natural wonders and beauty that are beyond the reaches of human imagination, and yet one so fraught with occurrences which spell disaster for all living beings – drought and flooding, earthquakes and tsunamis, the tumult of a planet which is in a state of perpetual flux. We try to find the logic in the suffering that seems to be such an inevitable part of human life, while all the time inwardly crying out against a divine being who could allow such pain and misery. We ask ourselves, openly or in the depths of our hearts, why good things happen to bad people, and trawl through books and media to find answers that will satisfy our deep feelings at the injustice of a world where innocent children suffer, good Christians are persecuted or our kindly neighbour suffers an agonisingly slow death from cancer.

This book does not hold the answers to these questions. But contentment in the face of suffering is not such a paradox as it seems; rather, it is something to be aimed for, if not always achieved.

Christian contentment is a belief in an all-loving God. It is the peace that is found in acknowledging that God's ways are not our ways. The fact that mystery is part of faith is not easily grasped, nor easily held on to. Such contentment is not the idleness of a mind which does not seek after the truth, preferring instead to push difficult questions aside and keep to the easy path. It is not the result of a timid faith which turns away from unpleasant enquiry for fear that the answers may not be there and that God is but a figment of a frightened imagination. Contentment comes from facing up to the difficult questions and digging deep into the mystery, discovering more about our faith and how it is to be lived out. Contentment comes from asking not that the cup of suffering is taken away from us, but that we may find the courage to accept what we cannot change and the grace to find God in the midst of the darkest places. Contentment comes from living in hope that at the end of time, all mysteries will be unveiled and we, who have been seeing things merely from the limited view of flawed human beings, will see through God's eyes, and all will be understood.

## Prayer

God, grant me the serenity to accept the things I cannot change, courage to change the things I can, and wisdom to know the difference.

Reinhold Niebuhr (1892–1971)

# We are never forsaken

He sustained him in a desert land, in a howling wilderness waste; he shielded him, cared for him, guarded him as the apple of his eye. As an eagle stirs up its nest, and hovers over its young; as it spreads its wings, takes them up, and bears them aloft on its pinions, the Lord alone guided him; no foreign god was with him. He set him upon the heights of the land, and fed him with produce of the field; he nursed him with honey from the crags, with oil from flinty rock; curds from the herd, and milk from the flock, with fat of lambs and rams; Bashan bulls and goats, together with the choicest wheat – you drank fine wine from the blood of grapes.

DEUTERONOMY 32:10–14

Again and again we hear it throughout the Old Testament, running like a golden thread through the multicoloured tapestry of stories of kings and beggars, prophets and priests, cities and fortresses, armies and farmers: the story of the deliverance of the children of Israel from slavery in Egypt. This story is integral to an understanding not only of the Old Testament, but of the New Testament as well. We must be familiar with the promises made by God to his people, the covenant he entered into with them, that they would be his children and he would be their God. We must tell and retell, to ourselves and to those around us, the stories of Noah and Abraham, of Moses and Joshua, the development of the covenant and its place within the hearts of the people. We must listen to the story of the journey to the promised land, of the years of wandering in the wilderness before the arrival at a land of milk and honey, of a people without a home given a place at last. For it is only by understanding all this that we can fully grasp the radical nature of Christ. It is only by knowing what went before that we can appreciate what is now: from the prophecy to the Word, from the ten stone tablets to the living embodiment of the covenant made flesh, from the promise to its fulfilment in all its glory. With the tearing of the veil of the temple, the way was opened to us, through the Way, Christ himself.

Those who walk in the Way are never alone, whether they are aware of it or not. When the path ahead seems dark, and it appears that everyone has deserted us, abandoning us to tread the road of suffering and pain by ourselves, still there is one who journeys beside us. Though we might not be aware of it, our footsteps are still guided. Though we feel as if our cries go unheard, yet there is one who hears them still and pays heed to them. We cannot know when we will reach the end of the dark places of our journey – we may emerge into sunlit meadows from the desert wilderness and rejoice in the light once more, finding ease and comfort in sun-warmed paths in the company of those we love, or we may only come into the light after we have entered the darkness of the great unknown, death itself. What we can know, with our hearts and souls, is that we will never be forsaken, that no step along the journey will be taken alone, that our travelling companion will always be by our side, because that has been promised to us from the beginning of time and will remain so until its very end: 'Be strong and bold; have no fear or dread of them, because it is the Lord your God who goes with you; he will not fail you or forsake you' (Deuteronomy 31:6).

## Exercise

'Footprints in the Sand' is a relatively recent poem. Its authorship is disputed, but it has nonetheless come to symbolise God's care for us at all times, even when we are not aware of it. It finds its roots in the promise of Deuteronomy 1:30–31:

> The Lord your God, who goes before you, is the one who will fight for you, just as he did for you in Egypt before your very eyes, and in the wilderness, where you saw how the Lord your God carried you, just as one carries a child, all the way that you travelled until you reached this place.

Write out or buy a copy of 'Footprints in the Sand' (you can find different versions of it online) or these verses from Deuteronomy, and keep it by you for when the times are hard.

# Section VIII

## Finding contentment

As we approach the end of our journey, we can look back and see how far we have travelled, all that we have learnt and the obstacles along the way which have been overcome. We cannot rest yet, however, as we are still on the road and must continue to focus. We continue to walk in faith, trusting in God's good purposes for us, even when the way forward seems unclear and the path full of difficulty. We give thanks to God for all that we see of his love in those around us, sharing the good news of Christ's love for all people, not just through what we say but also in our loving and generous actions towards our friends and neighbours, both near and far. We celebrate God's gifts to us and continue to use them to give to others, remaining faithful in prayer and service. And always we look to God, not allowing our good deeds to cloud our knowledge that the way to the Celestial City is not through works but by God's grace, freely offered to all.

# Give yourself to God

The hand of the Lord came upon me, and he brought me out by the spirit of the Lord and set me down in the middle of a valley; it was full of bones. He led me all round them; there were very many lying in the valley, and they were very dry. He said to me, 'Mortal, can these bones live?' I answered, 'O Lord God, you know.' Then he said to me, 'Prophesy to these bones, and say to them: O dry bones, hear the word of the Lord. Thus says the Lord God to these bones: I will cause breath to enter you, and you shall live. I will lay sinews on you, and will cause flesh to come upon you, and cover you with skin, and put breath in you, and you shall live; and you shall know that I am the Lord.'

EZEKIEL 37:1–6

The priest Ezekiel was the son of Buzi, who was probably also a priest. Taken captive in 597BC when the armies of Nebuchadnezzar, king of Babylon, captured Jerusalem, he was forced to leave the temple where he served and settle in Babylon, after which the temple itself was destroyed. This must have been devastating to a man such as Ezekiel, who had spent his life in service of the temple, not just because his role and position were taken from him, but because the very bedrock of his faith was threatened. For Ezekiel and the children of Israel, Jerusalem was Zion, the city of God himself. It was where God dwelt, and right in the heart of his dwelling place was the temple, the holy of holies, constructed by Solomon in accordance with God's direction. If the temple and the city were destroyed, where was God's dwelling place on earth? Had he abandoned his children? It is from the bleakness of not only a physical but also a spiritual exile that the prophet speaks. And he speaks in promises. Deprived of the structure that sustained his life, he must find a new way of thinking and believing. With the old supports destroyed, hope must be sought – and found – in a new place.

In the wilderness of exile, the children of Israel are nothing, like a heap of old bones left out to bleach in the sun, scattered and worthless. They can be brought together by Ezekiel, by the words of a priest, a leader, a prophet, but they are still lifeless: 'So I prophesied as I had been commanded; and as I prophesied, suddenly there was a noise, a rattling, and the bones came together, bone to its bone. I looked, and there were sinews on them, and flesh had come upon them, and skin had covered them; but there was no breath in them' (Ezekiel 37:7–8). It is not until God breathes upon the bones that they come to life: 'the breath came into them, and they lived, and stood on their feet, a vast multitude' (Ezekiel 37:10).

The breath of God gives hope and a future to the children of Israel. So too must we look to the breath of God to sustain us in all times and seasons, drawing in his love, dwelling on his promises, trusting in his support.

## Exercise

Take some time to focus on your own breath as it enters and leaves your body. You might find it helpful to do this simple breathing exercise.

Find a comfortable place to sit or lie – if this is not possible, find somewhere you can stand undisturbed for a short time. Make sure you feel supported and balanced in your body, relaxed but alert. Close your eyes if this helps.

Now move your attention to your breath, feeling it enter and leave your body, filling your body with life. Focus on the breath as it moves in and out. If your mind wanders, do not become anxious or concerned; simply take notice and return to the breath, in and out.

As you breathe out, you might like to say the word 'Yahweh', allowing it to become part of your exhalation. Let the breath become your prayer, your answering call to the reassurance and love of the breath of God as it fills your whole body: 'I will put my spirit within you, and you shall live' (Ezekiel 37:14).

# Walk in faith

'See, I have taught you statutes and rules, as the Lord my God commanded me, that you should do them in the land that you are entering to take possession of it. Keep them and do them, for that will be your wisdom and your understanding in the sight of the peoples, who, when they hear all these statutes, will say, "Surely this great nation is a wise and understanding people." For what great nation is there that has a god so near to it as the Lord our God is to us, whenever we call upon him? And what great nation is there, that has statutes and rules so righteous as all this law that I set before you today?

'Only take care, and keep your soul diligently, lest you forget the things that your eyes have seen, and lest they depart from your heart all the days of your life. Make them known to your children and your children's children.'

DEUTERONOMY 4:5–9 (ESV)

I can trace the beginnings of my journey to ordination when my third child was born. The legislation for the teaching of religion in schools had been changed, and Christian assemblies were no longer mandatory in church primary schools. Our Sunday school at the time was excellent, but it catered only for children of five years and older. It seemed to me that, following the recommendations of Deuteronomy, the earlier the better was the principle for teaching our children the stories of their faith. So my friend and I began a service for toddlers and their carers. I had no experience of teaching children, just a real passion for telling stories, so I learnt as I went along, helped by my friend who was a trained music teacher.

As time went on, I discovered and explored a vocation to the priest-hood, and in due course moved away from that church and served in other places. But my enthusiasm for sharing the stories of our faith has not diminished, and I continue to tell them – not just to children but in every context and to every type of audience. For if we do not have the examples of the Old Testament heroes, the letters to the newly formed churches, the songs of the psalms and, most of all, the life, death and resurrection of Jesus Christ in our hearts, then where do we turn when we are in need? If the sayings of Christ are woven into the very fabric of our lives, then it will become progressively harder to go against them. If we are so saturated in the word of God that it informs every word and gesture, then those words and gestures will become filled with the love and worship which is life itself. It is from a deep familiarity with the words and actions of Christ that we will draw the strength to continue when times are challenging. It is by reminding ourselves of his words of comfort and his attention to the suffering that we will ourselves find comfort, and it is through his promises that we will find hope for the future.

## Exercise

If you already have a pattern of studying and learning by heart phrases and passages from the Bible, then congratulations! If you do not, then why not begin the discipline of trying to learn by rote the passages which you find most helpful in your daily reading? Some people find that fitting them to music is very helpful. A lot of children's songs are available which teach both the passage and the reference in a lively way which is easy to remember – I still have fresh in my mind the songs I taught the toddlers over 20 years ago! Listen to them on the internet, find CDs in your local Christian bookshop or ask the person responsible for children's work in your church for recommendations.

Set a target for yourself of how many you will learn per week. Even if you commit simply to learning one Bible quote per week, by the end of a year you will have 52 valuable resources to draw on when you need them. Try to vary the type of quotation – some that refer to God's promises to us, for example, while others that give courage and hope in difficult times and others still that simply praise God for his love for all creation.

# Servants of God

As we work together with him, we urge you also not to accept the grace of God in vain. For he says, 'At an acceptable time I have listened to you, and on a day of salvation I have helped you.' See, now is the acceptable time; see, now is the day of salvation! We are putting no obstacle in anyone's way, so that no fault may be found with our ministry, but as servants of God we have commended ourselves in every way: through great endurance, in afflictions, hardships, calamities, beatings, imprisonments, riots, labours, sleepless nights, hunger; by purity, knowledge, patience, kindness, holiness of spirit, genuine love, truthful speech, and the power of God; with the weapons of righteousness for the right hand and for the left; in honour and dishonour, in ill repute and good repute. We are treated as impostors, and yet are true; as unknown, and yet are well known; as dying, and see – we are alive; as punished, and yet not killed; as sorrowful, yet always rejoicing; as poor, yet making many rich; as having nothing, and yet possessing everything.

2 CORINTHIANS 6:1–10

For as long as I have had a room to call my own, I have worked out my stress or anxiety through cleaning. It has some advantages as a reaction to worrying times and events, because even when everything else seems to be going wrong, at least the carpet has been hoovered! It is not always the most productive reaction, in that the problems may have nothing to do with the situation of my laundry, but I find that doing routine domestic tasks allows my mind time to find solutions when it otherwise might not or to reach an acceptance of a situation which cannot be solved by my own actions. The family can gauge how serious a matter is by what sort of cleaning I do – when I attack the oven, they know to keep out of my way until the problem is solved!

As I have written more than once in this book, the path of contentment is not easy. When we are faced with difficulties; when those around us or we ourselves suffer for no apparent reason; when we find the business of worship dreary and uninspiring; when our discipline of Bible study and prayer is hard work – all these times can make the journey challenging and the way forward uncomfortable. These reasons are all valid and respectable – the obstacles are genuine and some of them are beyond our control. But there will be other times, just as challenging, when our contentment is threatened for much less serious reasons, but which can, for all their apparent frivolity, seriously threaten the success of our journey.

When we are stricken with envy at the apparent good luck or success – deserved or otherwise – of someone we know; when we are consumed with longing for expensive or luxurious items which we cannot afford; when we are attracted to those whose lifestyle or life circumstances make a relationship inappropriate or simply wrong – then we will find the way to contentment just as challenging as if we were faced with a life-altering illness or situation.

The apostle Paul knows that the going will be tough sometimes, and although the challenges he describes are serious indeed, the advice he offers is nonetheless applicable to more minor situations. Simply put, we remember that we are 'servants of God', and as such will find satisfaction in carrying out those services for others which most benefit them. In undertaking to serve others, we will find a distraction for our worrying souls, will perhaps recognise the situation of others as more grave and serious than our own and will have achieved something far more useful than longing for things we cannot have or wishing we were in a different situation.

## Exercise

How do you react to times of worry and anxiety? Are these reactions useful, or do they cause more harm than good? Next time you feel under pressure, whether through being in a difficult situation or longing for life circumstances which are beyond your reach, try thinking of ways this anxiety and fretting can be turned to service for others. Offer to clean the church, cook a meal or bake a cake for a neighbour, or simply sign your name on a rota for an act of service for your community.

**45**

# Give thanks to the Lord

Sing to the Lord, all the earth. Tell of his salvation from day to day. Declare his glory among the nations, his marvellous works among all the peoples. For great is the Lord, and greatly to be praised; he is to be revered above all gods. For all the gods of the peoples are idols, but the Lord made the heavens. Honour and majesty are before him; strength and joy are in his place.

Ascribe to the Lord, O families of the peoples, ascribe to the Lord glory and strength. Ascribe to the Lord the glory due his name; bring an offering, and come before him. Worship the Lord in holy splendour; tremble before him, all the earth. The world is firmly established; it shall never be moved. Let the heavens be glad, and let the earth rejoice, and let them say among the nations, 'The Lord is king!' Let the sea roar, and all that fills it; let the field exult, and everything in it. Then shall the trees of the forest sing for joy before the Lord, for he comes to judge the earth. O give thanks to the Lord, for he is good; for his steadfast love endures forever.

1 CHRONICLES 16:23–34

'What is the chief end of man?' 'Man's chief end is to glorify God and enjoy him forever.'

So reads the first question of the Westminster Shorter Catechism, a series of questions and answers published in 1647 by the Westminster Assembly, a meeting of Scottish and English theologians designed to bring the two churches closer together in teaching. The catechism was aimed at children and those just beginning to discover their faith, and was also the basis for the teaching and preaching of the local church. It is now largely forgotten, except for this first question, which places worship right at the heart of Christian practice. Before we examine our consciences, before we bring before God the needs of the world and of ourselves, before we read and study the scriptures, we gather to glorify God.

Once again, we are reminded that in order to attain contentment, in order to live Christian lives of love and service and in order to be right with God, we must make the main thing the main thing – and the main thing is glorifying God. It is rejoicing in his power, in his infinite care for the whole of creation, the very creation he himself was involved in at the beginning and will remain completely involved with until the end of time. It is setting aside our own cares and anxieties, our triumphs and joys, putting them all out of our minds so that we can focus on the one who made us and whose love for us is more perfect and complete than we will ever know while we are on this earth.

Glorifying God, offering praise and worship to the one who created the world and holds the universe in his hands, is a discipline and a joy. It should be on our hearts first thing in the morning and last thing at night; it should be our priority during all times and seasons, in every situation. And very often this act of glorifying will rebound on us. As we lift up our hearts and minds to God in praise, we will find ourselves becoming comforted and supported in that very act. Our problems will achieve a better proportion, we will be reminded that there is one who is in control and whose good purposes for us cannot be doubted, and we will remember that God wants the best for each one of us for all time.

# Exercise

Make sure that your daily time of reflection and prayer, study and reading, begins and ends in praise. Spend time thanking God for his act of creation, sing songs or read passages from the psalms out loud to remind yourself of God's goodness. Psalms 145—150, the last five in the book, are psalms of praise which can be read out loud – Psalm 150 especially is short enough to be easily learned by heart!

# Consider the lilies

'Therefore I tell you, do not worry about your life, what you will eat or what you will drink, or about your body, what you will wear. Is not life more than food, and the body more than clothing? Look at the birds of the air; they neither sow nor reap nor gather into barns, and yet your heavenly Father feeds them. Are you not of more value than they? And can any of you by worrying add a single hour to your span of life? And why do you worry about clothing? Consider the lilies of the field, how they grow; they neither toil nor spin, yet I tell you, even Solomon in all his glory was not clothed like one of these... So do not worry about tomorrow, for tomorrow will bring worries of its own. Today's trouble is enough for today.'
MATTHEW 6:25–29, 34

I was at a particularly lengthy Christmas party, invited, I was sure, to make up the numbers, since an outbreak of flu had laid low a good proportion of the village population. Standing in a queue for food, the small boy in front of me – a grandson of the host – turned to me and said with complete seriousness, 'Are you rich?' I considered this carefully, and then replied that although in some people's eyes I was not particularly rich, I nonetheless counted myself fortunate in that I had enough money not to worry about where my next meal was coming from or to be concerned that I might lose the house I was living in. Warming to my theme, I added that I considered myself truly rich in terms of my relationships and in my job satisfaction. To all of this, the child paid little regard, simply staring at me and waiting for me to finish, whereupon he stated, 'I am rich. And I will be richer when my grandfather dies.' Nonplussed, I said nothing, but reflected on an attitude of privilege and the potential cost of such expectations.

It is very easy to focus on what we do not have, rather than the riches with which we have been blessed. As the saying goes, 'The VW Polo owner in a street full of bicycles considers himself fortunate; the same owner in a street full of BMWs considers himself poor indeed.' The powerful admonition in today's passage gets to the heart of Jesus' message; even if we had nothing more, we should count ourselves lucky that we have heard the gospel and know of Jesus' saving action in the world. But the fact is that we do have more. Our anxieties over the future are groundless, we are told, since we are in God's care, and he will do all that is necessary for us.

Contented living means thanking God for the gifts with which he has surrounded us – for the material necessities we need and for the emotional and spiritual support and comfort we receive. Contentment is achieved by grateful appreciation of the beauties that surround us: the changing seasons as they are reflected in our neighbourhood landscape; the signs of love we witness in the people with whom we share our lives; the message of hope which is brought to us daily through our reading and prayer. Casting aside unnecessary anxiety about the future, we live hopefully in the present, grateful for each moment and experiencing it to the full.

## Exercise

Make a 'blessings tree'. Either download a picture of a bare-branched tree from the internet or draw the outline of one on a large piece of paper. Take a separate sheet of paper and cut it into squares or circles, small enough to fit on the tree. If you can find a sheet of stickers, that would be even better – a set of colourful, decorative stickers better still!

Give yourself five minutes to write on the shapes all the blessings in your life. Be as imaginative as you can – don't stick simply to 'food' and 'clothing', but try to conjure those items of clothing which you appreciate, such as the warmth of a woolly scarf on a cold day or the taste of ice cream on a hot one. Remember to include spiritual and emotional blessings as well as material ones – 'a quiet place to pray' or 'being able to phone my friend whenever I need a chat'.

Decorate your tree with your stickers and see how full the tree is and how many blessings are in your life. You might wish to add more blessings as you think of them – or even more trees!

# Walking through the valley of the shadow of death

**The Lord is my shepherd, I shall not want. He makes me lie down in green pastures; he leads me beside still waters; he restores my soul. He leads me in right paths for his name's sake. Even though I walk through the darkest valley, I fear no evil; for you are with me; your rod and your staff – they comfort me. You prepare a table before me in the presence of my enemies; you anoint my head with oil; my cup overflows. Surely goodness and mercy shall follow me all the days of my life, and I shall dwell in the house of the Lord my whole life long.**

PSALM 23

This beautiful and familiar psalm has been one of the building blocks of faith for countless thousands of people as they have encountered the events and incidents of life. I have sat by the bedsides of the dying and recited this psalm, slowly and clearly, and seen how the lips of the elderly and very sick have moved, shaping the words which they do not have the strength to utter out loud but which still bring precious support. I have sung it in times of mourning, both individual and corporate, at funerals and on Remembrance Sunday. But I have also heard it, sung it and chanted it in celebration, as people gather together to commemorate joyous events: the dedication of a new community building, the arrival of a new parish priest, at weddings and baptisms. These few verses – so easily memorised, so adaptable to music – contain the pattern not just for our worship but for our lives, as they affirm their confidence in the goodness of the Lord God, who not only accompanies each one of us on our life's journey but also ensures that our direction and our destination is the right one for us.

Wherever we are led by life's events, or wherever our own wilful souls may take us, we will find the necessary support and help when we need it. We will be led through green valleys and experience times of great joy, but we will also encounter dark valleys and fearful times. Even then, we do not need to be concerned, because we are where God has led us and we are where we need to be. We might not know the reasons why, but we can trust in God's good purpose for us. We have been led into the valley by the good shepherd, in whom we can place all our faith. Like a flock of sheep, we may have to be guided through the valley of the shadow of death, dark and narrow as it is, surrounded by high walls of rock which block out the sun, making strange shadows leap and twist in front of us and behind us, so that we can arrive at the sunlit meadows and rivers in the next valley. Here the grass is green and we can rest and be restored, sharing joyfully in the feast of the kingdom which has been prepared for us, our cups overflowing and our plates piled high.

Thus the road to contentment is one we are happy to travel, whatever the landscape through which it passes, as we can be confident that we are where God means us to be and that the destination is always the house of the Lord.

## Exercise

Go for a walk. Taking a copy of this psalm with you, walk slowly and mindfully through your favourite landscape. If you are good at route-planning, try to include the different landscape features in your journey which match the ones in the psalm. Take a path that leads through a landscape which refreshes your soul – this may not be the green fields and still waters of the psalm, but something that appeals to you personally. It may take you past your local church, through a lively shopping quarter or simply along a familiar neighbourhood path. Try to follow this stretch with a section that is less appealing, mirroring the 'darkest valley'. Walk through your own 'darkest valley', remembering God's presence with you and his good purposes for you. Finally, end your journey at your favourite place, the one which reflects your vision of the 'house of the Lord'.

# After two whole years

When his master heard the words that his wife spoke to him, saying, 'This is the way your servant treated me,' he became enraged. And Joseph's master took him and put him into the prison, the place where the king's prisoners were confined; he remained there in prison. But the Lord was with Joseph and showed him steadfast love; he gave him favour in the sight of the chief jailer. The chief jailer committed to Joseph's care all the prisoners who were in the prison, and whatever was done there, he was the one who did it. The chief jailer paid no heed to anything that was in Joseph's care, because the Lord was with him; and whatever he did, the Lord made it prosper... After two whole years, Pharaoh dreamed.

GENESIS 39:19–23, 41:1

The story of Joseph is full of incident and adventure. The spoiled favourite son, his one redeeming feature his lifelong faith in God, the young Joseph is sold into slavery by his jealous brothers. His diligent and conscientious approach to his work wins the approval of his master Potiphar, who puts him in charge of his household. This comfortable position is wrested from him by the machinations of Potiphar's wife, who is angered at Joseph's refusal to sleep with her, and he is thrown into jail. But even there, Joseph is given responsibilities equal to his upright behaviour and his willingness to work hard at whatever task is given to him. His subsequent interpretation of Pharaoh's dreams restores him to his previous high position, from where he is able to prepare the country against famine and rescue his own family when they come to him in need.

A tale of triumph indeed – of honesty and integrity combined with a steadfast faith in God through all successes and disasters. But how easy it is to ignore the hardships which Joseph faced and focus instead on the glories of his position. One of the most poignant lines of the whole narrative is the first line of chapter 41, just before Joseph interprets Pharaoh's dream for him: 'after two whole years'. Four simple words, easily missed, but what must have been contained in the experience of those two years? That is 730 days of imprisonment, of hoping for release but fearing further reprisals, of being unable to move about freely, despite the rewards of responsibility given to him by the prison guards. What fortitude Joseph showed, to keep his faith in God, to maintain his integrity, to continue to carry out the tasks allotted to him!

The example of others who have lived through times of difficulty or danger should not be underestimated. From the personalities in the Bible – such as Paul and David, Samson and Joseph, Ruth and Naomi – from whom we learn so much, to present-day living examples of courage and hope in the face of disaster, we should not be too proud to take from the pattern of their lives a template for our own. Characters in books, whether real or fictional, whose ways of dealing with adversity offer us a method of coping with our own challenges; or support groups whose members share an experience out of which they offer advice to others in a similar situation – we are surrounded by examples on which we can model our own lives. Let us not be too proud to learn from them, whoever they are. Let us be sensitive to the 'two whole years' which they may have suffered before emerging with their personal brand of wisdom and experience that they might offer to others. Let us take courage and hope from the countless Josephs who have faced difficulties and emerged triumphant.

## Exercise

Make a stained-glass window of your 'saints'. Draw the shape of a simple stained-glass window on to black card – it need be no more than a simple arched window, but you can cut out smaller divisions within it if you wish to make it more complex.

To fill in your window, glue a sheet of plain paper to one side of the window frame. Write the names of the people whose lives have been an example to you in black ink in the spaces, and put the picture in your prayer space as a reminder to thank God for the examples of others and to try to live as an example to others yourself.

If you wish, you can make a more complex window. Use coloured tissue paper or cellophane instead of plain paper for the window 'glass', or simply wipe over the plain paper with a small amount of cooking oil on a piece of cotton wool. This will make the paper translucent and show up the names more clearly.

# Friend, move up higher

When he noticed how the guests chose the places of honour, he told them a parable. 'When you are invited by someone to a wedding banquet, do not sit down at the place of honour, in case someone more distinguished than you has been invited by your host; and the host who invited both of you may come and say to you, "Give this person your place", and then in disgrace you would start to take the lowest place. But when you are invited, go and sit down at the lowest place, so that when your host comes, he may say to you, "Friend, move up higher"; then you will be honoured in the presence of all who sit at the table with you. For all who exalt themselves will be humbled, and those who humble themselves will be exalted.'

LUKE 14:7–11

Some years ago, at the beginning of my ordained ministry, I worked with a British Army chaplain, caring for two regiments in the south of England. This was exciting and adventurous work, and it gave me valuable insight into the nature and demands of chaplaincy. I was invited to accompany one of the regiments on exercise in Scotland and was informed that I would be collected at 6.00 am. This was not a struggle as I had three young children at the time, and on some days 6.00 am felt like almost lunchtime! The day came, and an army Land Rover drew up outside my door, and four soldiers in full military kit stepped out along with the chaplain. I, on my side, was accompanied by three small children and a husband still wearing his pyjamas, which were tastefully patterned with teddy bears wearing pompom hats. I saw the smirks on the faces of the soldiers as they studied him, and the way he noticed this and happily ignored it, waving goodbye as I was driven off to the wilds of the Scottish hills.

Reflecting on this behaviour, I realised that to wear teddy-bear pyjamas when faced with fully dressed soldiers required an inner certainty and confidence which was truly significant. It never crossed my husband's mind to 'compete' in any way with these soldiers, because he knew who he was – and who he was not. He has kept this precious quality throughout his life. He is happy to be valued and treated as an honoured guest, and equally happy to be ignored and pushed to the bottom end of the table. Where he is seated, physically or metaphorically, does not affect his assessment of himself or his relationship with others – he treats all as his equals, whether society views them as such or not.

This gift is available to all who seek it, to all who find their value in their preciousness to God, in their relationships with others and in their service to their community. Most of all, it is given to those who seek within themselves that true humility which acknowledges that everything we have and all that we are is not a possession we may hold on to, but a gift given to us by God, to be used for the benefit of others.

## Exercise: a litany for humility

Lord Jesus, meek and humble of heart, *Hear me.*

From the desire of being esteemed, *Deliver me, Jesus.*
From the desire of being loved, *Deliver me, Jesus.*
From the desire of being extolled, *Deliver me, Jesus.*
From the desire of being honoured, *Deliver me, Jesus.*
From the desire of being praised, *Deliver me, Jesus.*
From the desire of being preferred to others, *Deliver me, Jesus.*
From the desire of being consulted, *Deliver me, Jesus.*
From the desire of being approved, *Deliver me, Jesus.*

From the fear of being humiliated, *Deliver me, Jesus.*
From the fear of being despised, *Deliver me, Jesus.*
From the fear of suffering rebukes, *Deliver me, Jesus.*
From the fear of being calumniated, *Deliver me, Jesus.*
From the fear of being forgotten, *Deliver me, Jesus.*
From the fear of being ridiculed, *Deliver me, Jesus.*
From the fear of being wronged, *Deliver me, Jesus.*
From the fear of being suspected, *Deliver me, Jesus.*

That others may be loved more than I,
*Jesus, grant me the grace to desire it.*
That others may be esteemed more than I,
*Jesus, grant me the grace to desire it.*
That, in the opinion of the world, others may increase and I may
   decrease,
*Jesus, grant me the grace to desire it.*
That others may be chosen and I set aside,
*Jesus, grant me the grace to desire it.*
That others may be praised and I unnoticed,
*Jesus, grant me the grace to desire it.*
That others may be preferred to me in everything,
*Jesus, grant me the grace to desire it.*
That others may become holier than I, provided that I may become
   as holy as I should,
*Jesus, grant me the grace to desire it.*

# A new commandment

'Little children, I am with you only a little longer. You will look for me; and as I said to the Jews so now I say to you, "Where I am going, you cannot come." I give you a new commandment, that you love one another. Just as I have loved you, you also should love one another. By this everyone will know that you are my disciples, if you have love for one another.'

JOHN 13:33–35

It is well known that Jesus had no settled home during his ministry (see page 79), and we know that he spent time alone, some of it a deliberate stepping aside but some of it forced upon him. During his times of greatest trial, in the wilderness and at his arrest, the fact that he endured these occasions alone is emphasised in the gospel, adding as it does to his sufferings. But this does not mean that he lived without companionship. During his time of preaching and teaching, he gathered around him a group of people for mutual support and learning. They were a disparate group, to be sure, and this must have at times made for arguments and disagreements, but their very difference would have ensured that each brought their own gifts and abilities to the group, complementing the others for the benefit of the whole.

Recent research has shown that people live longer if they are engaged with others in some way – whether in their local communities, through membership of groups or societies or simply by being involved in caring for their wider family. More importantly, perhaps, people are happier and feel more fulfilled if they have a good social network. This has become recognised on a national level with the appointment of a minister for loneliness, whose role is to address the issues of the two million people over 75 who are living alone and the more than nine million who are affected by loneliness.

One of the roles of Christians in their communities is to acknowledge and reinforce the value of companionship, reaching out to each other in love and care. There will be frictions and disagreements – there always are when human beings gather together – but any group will grow stronger if these potential disruptions to harmony are treated with respect, tolerance and a keen desire to work together for a solution. One of the greatest gifts we can give to another is that of simple recognition – acknowledging their existence on this planet, respecting their lives and their experience, valuing them for who they are and thanking them for it. It is in small, simple ways that we build up Christ's kingdom – in smiling and saying hello to the stranger, looking out for the neighbour who lives alone, noticing the life events of those around us and acknowledging them. We do this without looking for reciprocation, but that will come naturally, for love grows as it is shared. And slowly, and gently, the presence of Christ becomes known: 'Where two or three are gathered together in my name, there am I in the midst of them' (Matthew 18:20, KJV).

## Exercise

Try today to greet a stranger, to listen to a friend, to invite a neighbour or colleague to an event, to start a conversation or to compliment someone on something they have said or done. As Mother Teresa said: 'We can do no great things; only small things with great love.'

**51**

# I can do all things

I rejoice in the Lord greatly that now at last you have revived your concern for me; indeed, you were concerned for me, but had no opportunity to show it. Not that I am referring to being in need; for I have learned to be content with whatever I have. I know what it is to have little, and I know what it is to have plenty. In any and all circumstances I have learned the secret of being well-fed and of going hungry, of having plenty and of being in need. I can do all things through him who strengthens me.

PHILIPPIANS 4:10–13

And so here we are, back at the beginning, with the same passage that we started with (page 14), our journey almost complete, but still with so much to learn.

You would not know, would you, that the writer of Philippians was in prison? You would not know that he had suffered all sorts of punishments and indignities, nor that he would eventually be executed for his faith. You would not know that he was writing to a group of people who were being harassed and persecuted because they were Christians and would soon be facing even more extreme measures to prevent them from practising their faith. This passage is filled with joy, hope and a sense that whatever the future holds, the writer will be equal to it, because his certainty is centred not within himself and his own abilities, but in God, who holds his future in love.

This hope is not an empty one, but one based on previous experience, on the testimony of others and on a faith lived out in the most extreme circumstances. But it is also the hope born of a choice made deliberately by the writer, Paul, himself. He could have chosen to be bitter, to write in despairing terms about all the hardships that had happened to him and about the bleakness of the future that he and the people of Philippi undoubtedly faced. But he doesn't – he focuses on the positive points, and his letter is alive with his determination to make the most of the gifts that have been given to him and to use them in service to God. 'I have learned the secret,' he writes, and we too are learning that secret – which is to be content with whatever befalls us, because we trust that God is in charge of the outcome. We are learning the secret of being grateful for all that we have been given, for living in grateful expectation of future grace. We are learning that, although we may not always be able to decide what will happen to us, we can all determine how we will respond to that which has happened – and that response must be rooted and grounded in love.

'I can do all things,' writes the prisoner, the shipwrecked one, the beaten, starved and tortured one. 'I can do all things' because I live not in my own strength but in the strength of the one who created me. 'I can do all things' because life itself is a gift, not a right; a privilege, not a debt owed to me. 'I can do all things' because the weaker and more flawed I am, the more the grace of God shines through me; the less confident I am in my own strength, the more the strength of God sustains me. 'I can do all things... through him who strengthens me.'

## Exercise

Philippians 4:13 is known as the 'ten-finger prayer', as each word corresponds to the fingers of both hands.

Instead of counting to ten in times of anger or stress, try taking a deep breath and counting off this prayer on your fingers, one by one. Do this as many times as you need, allowing the meaning of the words to sink into your heart.

From time to time during the day, stretch out your hands in front of you, fingers apart, and remind yourself of the gift of life which has been given to you and the power you hold to share that gift with those you meet.

# The end of the journey?

Then I saw a new heaven and a new earth; for the first heaven and the first earth had passed away, and the sea was no more. And I saw the holy city, the new Jerusalem, coming down out of heaven from God, prepared as a bride adorned for her husband. And I heard a loud voice from the throne saying, 'See, the home of God is among mortals. He will dwell with them; they will be his peoples, and God himself will be with them; he will wipe every tear from their eyes. Death will be no more; mourning and crying and pain will be no more, for the first things have passed away.'

And the one who was seated on the throne said, 'See, I am making all things new.' Also he said, 'Write this, for these words are trustworthy and true.' Then he said to me, 'It is done! I am the Alpha and the Omega, the beginning and the end. To the thirsty I will give water as a gift from the spring of the water of life. Those who conquer will inherit these things, and I will be their God and they will be my children.'

REVELATION 21:1–7

And so we come to the end of the journey, as we gaze at the picture of a heaven and earth 'made new', given to us with such poetry and longing by the visionary John, who is writing in the midst of terror and persecution, when it seemed that heaven-on-earth was very far away indeed, and mourning and crying and pain were the order of the day.

Except – we are not at the end of the journey, because although we have studied and read and reflected and practised for over 50 days, we have not arrived. The journey of faith, the journey to contentment, is as long as the journey of our lives, ending only when we arrive at our eternal home, prepared so lovingly for us by Christ, who has gone before us for that very purpose. Hopefully structures will be in place, disciplines accepted and practices established that will help us in our quest for contentment, but like most skills, it is not enough merely to set them up; they must be kept up if they are to accomplish their intention.

Above all, our hearts and minds must be nurtured, nourished and kept focused if we are to develop and grow the gift of contentment which we seek. Rewards will become apparent along the way, as our practice shows results, our lives become more settled and our souls are freed from the preoccupations which direct us away from our primary focus on God. But we must not cease until that final day, when we see 'face to face' that which for now we see 'in a mirror, darkly', when we 'know fully' even as we have been 'fully known' (1 Corinthians 13:12, ASV).

My prayers are for you as you continue on your journey.

Sally Welch explores the less-travelled pilgrim routes of the UK and beyond, through the eyes of the pilgrims who walk them. Each chapter explores a different aspect of pilgrimage, offering reflections and indicating some of the spiritual lessons to be learned that may be practised at home. This absorbing book shows how insights gained on the journey can be incorporated into the spiritual life of every day, bringing new ways of relationship with God and with our fellow Christians, offering support and encouragement as we face the joys and challenges of life.

**Pilgrim Journeys**
*Pilgrimage for walkers and armchair travellers*
Sally Welch

978 0 85746 513 9  £7.99

**brfonline.org.uk**

*New Daylight* offers four months of daily Bible reading and reflection for everybody who wants to go deeper with God. It is ideal for those looking for a fresh approach to regular Bible study, and offers a talented team of contributors who present a Bible passage (text included), helpful comment and a prayer or thought for the day ahead.

**New Daylight**
*Sustaining your daily journey with the Bible*
Edited by Sally Welch
£4.70 per issue

**brfonline.org.uk**

*Enabling all ages to grow in faith*

Anna Chaplaincy
Barnabas in Schools
Holy Habits
Living Faith
Messy Church
Parenting for Faith

**The Bible Reading Fellowship (BRF)** is a Christian charity that resources individuals and churches and provides a professional education service to primary schools.

Our vision is to enable people of all ages to grow in faith and understanding of the Bible and to see more people equipped to exercise their gifts in leadership and ministry.

**To find out more about our ministries and programmes, visit**

**brf.org.uk**